HEAVEN
TOUCHING
EARTH

Books Compiled by
James Stuart Bell

Angels, Miracles, and Heavenly Encounters
From the Library of A. W. Tozer
From the Library of Charles Spurgeon
Love Is a Flame
Love Is a Verb (with Gary Chapman)
Love Is a Verb Devotional (with Gary Chapman)

HEAVEN
TOUCHING
EARTH

True Stories *of* Angels, Miracles,
and Heavenly Encounters

COMPILED BY
JAMES STUART BELL

BETHANY HOUSE PUBLISHERS
a division of Baker Publishing Group
Minneapolis, Minnesota

© 2014 by Whitestone Communications, Inc.

Published by Bethany House Publishers
11400 Hampshire Avenue South
Bloomington, Minnesota 55438
www.bethanyhouse.com

Bethany House Publishers is a division of
Baker Publishing Group, Grand Rapids, Michigan

Printed in the United States of America

Library of Congress Cataloging-in-Publication Data
Heaven touching earth : true stories of angels, miracles, and heavenly encounters / compiled by James Stuart Bell.
    pages cm
    Summary: "A compilation of true stories of the supernatural—angels, miracles, and heavenly encounters—written from a Christian perspective"— Provided by publisher.
    ISBN 978-0-7642-1186-7 (pbk. : alk. paper)
    1. Angels—Christianity—Anecdotes. 2. Miracles—Anecdotes. 3. Supernatural—Anecdotes. 4. Christian life—Anecdotes. I. Bell, James S., compiler.
    BT966.3.H43 2014
    231.7′3—dc23   2014017434

The following are true stories, but some details and names have been changed in order to protect privacy.

Editorial services provided by Jeanette Gardner Littleton Publication Services

Cover design by Brand Navigation

15 16 17 18 19 20 21   8 7 6 5 4 3 2

To Tim Burt and Mark Reed,
two long-lost friends who,
through stories like these,
have been found

Contents

Acknowledgments 11

Introduction 13

Maureen and the Prophetess 17
GEORGE FERRER
•

The Car That Drove Itself 21
MARTIN ZIEGNER
•

The Mad Dog Who Cared 26
MARTHA NELSON
•

Angel on Route 495 33
SUSAN A. J. LYTTEK
•

Give God Time 38
JAMES STUART BELL
•

Bear Hugs in Heaven 44
G. L. FRANCIS
•

Getting the Blob off My Bed 51
INGRID SHELTON

•

Wings of Peace 55
CHERYL CHRISTENSEN JOHNSTON

•

The Total Package 59
JEANIE JACOBSON

•

No Longer Abandoned 64
JUDY HAMPTON

•

Who Has Seen the Wind? 72
BETTY JOHNSON DALRYMPLE

•

Glowing Red Eyes 77
LORETTA EIDSON

•

The Midnight Traveler 82
LINDA HOWTON, AS TOLD TO JOYCE GATTON

•

The Mysterious Blonde 87
M. JEANETTE SHARP

•

The Impotent Imp 92
JAN DIXON SYKES

•

The Angel on the Wall 96
CAROLYN D. POINDEXTER

•

Divine GPS 101
DALE L. DRAGOMIR

•

Shelter From the Storm 107
DEB WUETHRICH

•

A Two-Captive Release 111
P. R. JARAMILLO

•

Contents

The Moveable Moose   118
MARGARET ANN STIMATZ
•

Ex-Marlboro Man   122
JAMES STUART BELL
•

A Call Homeward   126
CHRISTINE HENDERSON
•

Multiplying the Strength He Gave Me   131
ANNETTE M. ECKART
•

A Boatload of Trouble   139
JUDY PARROTT
•

A Guy Named Andy   146
TIMOTHY J. BURT
•

The Scent of Blessing   152
DEB WUETHRICH
•

Nothing Is Incurable   159
MARTY PRUDHOMME
•

A Critical Left Turn   164
TRISH PROPSON
•

A New Creation   169
KELLY J. STIGLIANO
•

Penniless in Bangkok   173
SCOTI SPRINGFIELD DOMEIJ
•

The One-in-Three-Million Miracle   181
JAMES STUART BELL
•

The Still, Small Voice of Authority   187
DELORES CHRISTIAN LIESNER
•

Who's Behind the Wheel? 191
SHERYL K. JONES
•

Door-to-Door Surprise 195
JANICE RICE
•

Angel in the Mirror 201
SALLY EDWARDS DANLEY
•

Gracious Intervention 205
WALTER B. HUCKABY
•

Angels Are Watching Over Me 211
ALICE M. MCGHEE
•

The Key to God's Power 216
BOB HASLAM
•

God Protects the Weak 220
MARLENE ANDERSON
•

The Half-Mile Celestial Bowl 224
JOHN C. MANNONE
•

Don't Trust Bow, Sword, or Metal Door 230
SHERYL K. JONES
•

A Voice From Heaven 237
MONICA CANE
•

Holy Electricity 241
DELORES E. TOPLIFF

About the Contributors 247

Acknowledgments

Thanks to Kyle Duncan, now at Scriptorium, for his original idea for this series. Great appreciation for Andy McGuire for his enthusiasm and encouragement in bringing this to birth, to Ellen Chalifoux for her fine editorial skills, and for the background support of Carissa Maki and Brett Benson. Finally, thanks to friend Tim Peterson for his constant support of me as a contributor to the Bethany House list.

Introduction

At certain times in our lives heaven and earth can seem so far apart. When we are going through difficult times, heaven can seem like a remote and distant place, and God seems to be absent when we call. We know of loved ones who have gone on to be with the Lord—where there is no darkness, sickness, or failure—and perhaps we envy their "everlasting rest" and their joy and bliss as they experience the amazing perfections of heaven in ways of which we have no inkling.

Yet the kingdom of heaven is indeed in our midst, or as Jesus said, actually within us. We, in turn, are also mysteriously "seated in heavenly places" with Him. Though we can rarely see it or fully comprehend it, Jesus has brought heaven down to earth and reconciled us so that the barriers we often perceive are really nonexistent.

This volume is a collection of stories of when heaven and earth come together; it is a sequel to my first volume on this subject: *Angels, Miracles, and Heavenly Encounters*. There are similar stories of near-death experiences, encounters with angels, spiritual warfare, miracles, and other occurrences where only a supernatural explanation fits the circumstances.

As Christians, none of us is guaranteed any of these types of experiences no matter how good or needy we may be, and we are not inferior simply because we haven't experienced these things. We do not need "signs and wonders" to have a vibrant overcoming faith; God gives us everything we need as we receive Christ himself by faith on a daily basis. But for God's own mysterious and sovereign reasons, He does manifest himself in powerful supernatural displays. These build up all of us as they are shared, as God is revealed in new, exciting, and intimate ways consistent with His person and character.

If you talk to others in your church or with your Christian friends and family, you'll maybe find someone who has had a supernatural experience similar to those found in this book. Sometime, somewhere in the lives of these persons, God chose to manifest himself in an extraordinary way that can only be marveled at to the praise of His glory. As a result, their lives have been enriched; indeed, they might say their lives have never been the same.

God doesn't give these experiences because the subjects of these stories are superspiritual or church leaders, but rather, these pages are filled with ordinary believers who seek Him to simply be involved and answer their requests and needs. That's not to say that some of the circumstances here are not dramatic and desperate, for many are just that. You might want to say that God does extraordinary things in unusual circumstances in ordinary people. And that gives hope to you and me, for after reading these stories we may have greater expectations that we, too, may have an encounter with heaven while still on this earth.

James Stuart Bell

Maureen and the Prophetess

GEORGE FERRER

The bank was closing at three that afternoon, and as the manager of a business, I needed to make a deposit. As I looked at the clock, I realized that if I left at that moment, I would make it to the bank on time—if two of the three lights were green. I zoomed out the front door.

Our office door was solid wood and did not have a window. I usually exited the building cautiously in case a person was approaching the door from the outside, but this day I was rushing and almost knocked a woman into the bushes along the walkway near our door.

I stopped, frozen in surprise.

The woman stepped backward into the shrub bed. Her high heels sank into the rich soil, and she swayed back and forth, waving her arms to avoid falling into the bushes.

I felt embarrassed and amused, and she looked as if she felt the same. She was well dressed in business-casual clothing, her European sports car was parked at the curb, and her hair and makeup were flawless.

"I am sorry," I apologized, thinking she might be there for an appointment that had slipped my mind. "I must run out for a moment. If we can help you with anything, please ask Maureen for assistance."

She stared at me.

"What did you say?" she demanded.

It was my turn to be off balance—mentally, anyway. I reviewed my comment and my demeanor. Had I offended her because I was rushing off or embarrassed her by practically pushing her into the bushes?

"I am sorry I surprised you," I said. "I cannot stay and assist you, but Maureen is in the office and she can help you."

She stepped back onto the walkway to the office and straightened herself with a flourish.

"I just came to use the restroom," she said.

Then her demeanor changed.

"Did you just say I should talk to Maureen?" she almost shouted with excitement.

This was getting very strange. She stood ramrod straight like a woman with a life-or-death mission, and proclaimed, "All right, I will go talk to Maureen."

She marched into the office building.

She is pretty, but she is nuts, I thought as I jumped into my car and roared off to the bank. *Maureen will kill me when I get back. I just sent a mentally unbalanced person to talk to her, and she's not in any mood for a difficult customer.*

I knew Maureen was not ready to deal with a difficult customer, because the company had just closed Maureen's department and she was packing loose ends before leaving. She was smart and tough—a good team member and a great manager with excellent customer service skills. I had wanted her transferred to my department, but that request was denied, and Maureen was upset about leaving.

When I returned to my office with the deposit slip from the bank, the European sports car was gone.

But Maureen, despite her tough and resilient personality, was crying in a back office.

"Is that you, George?" Maureen asked as I rounded the counter separating the lobby from the customer service area. She added, "Did you send that woman to talk to me?"

I had never seen Maureen this unprofessional. With makeup smeared, hair out of place, and tears on her cheeks, she only glanced in my direction.

I braced myself for an emotional onslaught from Maureen, but her demeanor was meek.

"Do you know what that woman said to me?"

"I met her at the door on my way to the bank. I was in a rush and she had to use the ladies' room," I tried to explain. But Maureen was not listening to me.

"When she came out of the ladies' room, she asked if I was Maureen. I said yes, and she said she lives in Queens, about forty-five miles away, and she prays every morning. This morning the Lord told her to 'go to Maureen and tell her I love her, and tell her I, the Lord, have a plan for her life. She is going to have some very difficult and painful times, but if she trusts me, I will be with her through it all.'"

The woman that I now think of as "the prophetess" had continued to explain that she did not know anyone named Maureen. The only association with the name *Maureen* she could think of was a place called Maureen's Kitchen in the next town from our office.

Unsure of whom she was going to speak to or where she was going, she left home and headed to Maureen's Kitchen. But on the way, she had to use the ladies' room. She had stopped at our building, where she had run into me and learned there was a Maureen inside.

Maureen cried tears of joy and repentance. I rejoiced with her and made it a point to keep in contact with her and encourage her and her family through those difficult times. As the prophetess said, Maureen experienced much heartache and pain, but she walked with her Lord through it all, and during the worst of times we saw Maureen reconciled with her family and her church.

A year after Maureen left the company, I was transferred to another location and hired Maureen as a customer service representative. Sadly, cancer robbed her life too soon.

As I went to Maureen's burial, I realized her earthly body would rest only about three hundred feet from where she'd met the prophetess. But thanks to the prophetess being obedient to God's guidance, Maureen's spirit was now living with the God who'd promised to be with her.

The Car That Drove Itself

MARTIN ZIEGNER

M artin Luther King Jr. was shot on the evening of Thursday, April 4, 1968. The rioting that followed in Chicago over the next several days resulted in widespread looting, shootings, and fires on the south and west sides of the city.

I was a twenty-two-year-old student living on the near north side. I considered myself a Christian—I had grown up in a home that observed Christian holidays, went to church regularly, and had graduated from a Christian high school with a WWJD motif for viewing the world.

When I went to college, I thought I should examine other religious viewpoints and drifted into Zen Buddhism. By 1968 I was in grad school and had immersed myself in the culture of the day. I had spent Friday night of that week hanging out with friends and got up early on Saturday to go to my weekend job.

At this point I was not really aware of the extent of the disturbances going on around the city and headed west in my car along Division Street. As I approached LaSalle Street, I saw that the road about two hundred yards ahead of me was covered with debris—fires blazed in the street and quite a few people milled about, yelling, running, and throwing things. Normally on a Saturday morning the Cabrini-Green area was quiet—I had never had a problem driving through there. But that Saturday morning it was like a combat zone!

The light at LaSalle Street had turned red, and as I slowed to a stop I considered whether to turn left or right to avoid the area directly ahead of me. Then I saw a young black kid standing on the corner, holding on his right shoulder what seemed to be a package. I thought that he was waiting for the bus.

When he saw me, he yelled nasty things and ran toward my car. I saw that the package was actually a bowling-ball-sized piece of concrete. When he got about six feet from my car, he shot-putted the concrete directly at my front windshield.

Time seemed to slow to an absolute crawl. As I watched the piece of concrete tumbling toward my face, I could make out the fine structure of its surface illuminated by the morning sun. I felt something in my awareness split; the analytical part of my brain decided that I should deal with the situation by trying to figure out if the concrete was a sand mix or an aggregate of particles in composition. I decided it must be an aggregate.

Why is the surface sparkling? I wondered next. The analytical part of me considered, *Maybe it contains mica. No, wait, mica has slip planes. That can't be right. Oh wait, quartz. Yeah, quartz would work.*

The analytical side of me was very pleased and satisfied. (After all, I studied science in order to become a dentist.) Meanwhile, the emotional side of me felt like the figure in Edvard Munch's painting *The Scream.*

As the piece of concrete came closer, I heard a quiet, very calm voice say, "You know, if that hits you it will kill you!"

Oh yeah, right! I thought and hit pedal to the metal.

The car lurched forward and concrete exploded through the driver's-side rear window, showering glass throughout the car interior. The car went through the intersection and began traveling down Division Street, directly into the maelstrom of violence I had wanted to avoid. My response was to go into a state of shock—my hands fell off the steering wheel into my lap, my foot let off the gas pedal, and I just sat there, gaping and frozen.

I could not move a muscle.

My car continued slowly down the street—with no one driving. On my left, a woman was walking down the sidewalk in the direction I was going. As I drew abreast of her, she turned and stared intently into a store—she did not see my car.

At this time I felt something like a weight settle onto the car—it seemed like there suddenly wasn't as much headroom as there had been a moment earlier. But it wasn't just a weight—it felt alive, aware, intelligent, personal, loving, and completely in control, whereas I had no control—I could not move. No one was driving; my foot was not on the gas.

As the car drove over scattered debris, I could hear glass bottles breaking and knew that this would be a bad time to get a blowout!

On my right, two looters came running out of a store carrying a couch—one was running backwards at the end of the couch closest to me, and the man at the other end suddenly dropped the couch and immediately spun around to his right. He walked back to the store, yelling and gesturing. Neither of them reacted to my car passing within a few feet of them.

The street was now thick with debris—bricks, bottles, pieces of wood, and junk. Straight ahead of me was a fifty-five-gallon drum filled with a fire that was burning whatever was thrown into it. My car was bumping across the debris— the steering wheel jerking wildly from side to side—and I was still frozen in place.

Then I became aware that the ground around the car didn't look right. At the time I had no words to describe what I was seeing, but now I would describe it as pixelated—like when a TV signal is not decoded properly.

I was terrified that I would run into the burning drum and the car would stop or that the tires would finally blow out on the broken glass. To my amazement, the wildly jerking steering wheel steered the car by itself around the drum—first to the left and then back into the street.

To my horror, another burning drum loomed ahead, belching black smoke.

Again, the interaction between the debris and the wheels appeared to steer the car around the drum and back down the street.

At this point my car crossed the Chicago River into an industrial area that appeared deserted—the ground stopped pixelating and the car slowed to a stop. The sense of weight on the car and me lifted, and I found that I could move and start driving again. Later I measured the distance that my car had traveled without me as the driver: over four thousand feet—nearly a mile.

All I wanted to do was to get out of this very dangerous area. So I drove to work, brushing the pieces of glass out of my hair and clothes. I thought I was losing my mind—I was terrified by what had just happened, and at the same time I wanted to go back to being in the grasp of that Presence that had settled over me. I had a precious experience of being rescued from truly dire circumstances by a Presence that was so palpable and loving, so stupefyingly powerful and in complete control of this desperate situation.

At the time I could not understand why He would save me—it took a long time for me to understand that God does what He does because it pleases Him and He answers to no one. There is no question in my mind that His angels surrounded and drove my car that day of the Chicago riots. They were holding me up "lest I catch my foot upon a stone"—the stones and debris that could have seriously hurt or even killed me. Today I think of the verse "Be still, and know that I am God" (Psalm 46:10)—His wonderful gift of peace to me, knowing that He is in control of all my circumstances.

The Mad Dog
Who Cared

MARTHA NELSON

Mr. Brewster, I need to go home."

My teacher looked up from the stack of papers yet to be graded. "What seems to be the problem?"

"I'm sick to my stomach." I said it quietly so my classmates wouldn't hear.

"Well, Martha, I'll need to call your parents."

I glanced at the class. They all seemed busy with our history assignment. "We don't have a phone on Big Island." I hoped none of them heard. At twelve, I was old enough to be embarrassed about my family's finances. Even more quietly I added, "We were supposed to get one when the electricity got hooked up. But Papa's been out of work."

I stared at the floor, not wanting to have to say more.

"How do you expect to get home, then?"

"I'll walk."

He took off his glasses and put them on the desk. "Young lady, do you have any idea how far it is to Big Island?"

"Yes, sir." My chin went up. "I walk four miles here every day. But it's only two miles to Vine Hill. That's where my brother Bob is working. He'll take me home—he has his car."

"How about if you just lie down for a while? See if you feel better."

"No, thank you. My mom will know what to do."

Mr. Brewster shook his head. "All right. It seems you've got everything worked out. The frontage road has fewer cars, so go that way." He looked toward the window. "And it's snowing, so bundle up."

The full force of the wind didn't hit me until I rounded the corner of the school. The radio had said nothing about snow today. I shivered, pulled my wool cap over my ears, and fastened the top button of my jacket.

I don't remember much about the walk to Vine Hill except the dropping temperatures and my stomachache. But I can't forget how my heart sank when I reached the construction site and the lone car there was not my brother's. Only the sheet-metal worker answered when I called out.

"You're looking for Bob Nelson?" the man said from the top of the stairway. "I'm the only one left. Everyone else went home because of the storm."

I forgot about being sick. Should I retrace the two miles to school or go on? From Vine Hill, home was about five miles.

I'd still have to cross the ice to Big Island. But I had walked it daily since the lake had frozen. I felt confident I could do it myself.

On top of Vine Hill, no trees shielded me from the cold wind. I wrestled along for half a mile, sometimes walking backward. Soon I could hardly see the road ahead. This was no ordinary snowfall—it had become a blinding blizzard.

As I turned onto County Road, something nudged my leg. I looked down and saw a scrawny white terrier. He wagged his tail.

"Where did you come from? What are you doing out in this storm?"

I surprised myself—normally I was afraid of strange dogs. "You poor thing, you look half starved. I'm sorry I don't have any food for you."

I started off again and he stayed with me.

"Don't you have a home?" I asked.

His eyes—I'd never seen one of our dogs look like that. He earnestly fixed his eyes on me as if he wanted to say something. I turned back into the wind. The dog struggled through the storm at my side for two and a half miles to Windsor. At times the wind snatched the breath out of my mouth. The dog and I put our heads down and pressed against the gusts.

As we trudged forward, I envisioned the route ahead of me. At the edge of Lake Minnetonka, I reasoned that if I could keep my eyes on the spot where I knew the island was, I could make it the last two miles across the ice to our bay. If I could just keep my eyes straight ahead and not look away for even an instant, I wouldn't become disoriented by the blowing snow. Papa had warned us kids many times about the danger of losing our way in the snow.

I never dreamed the dog would follow me onto the ice, but I felt glad for his company when he did.

On the ice, winter's full blast lashed us. We hadn't even gotten halfway across the lake when the dog suddenly turned on me. He bit at my ankles in a frenzy, barking and growling. He had gone mad!

What would I do? I tried to shake him off, but I was terrified to move my eyes from my focal point, my only hope to get myself home.

"Get off! What's the matter with you?" I screamed. He continued to attack me. I had no choice but to break my focus and look down.

That's when I saw it. Open water. One step was all there was between the open water and me. The dog's attack ceased. I inched backward. He followed me, quiet. I sat on the ice and put my shaking arms around the strange little dog that had just saved my life.

I don't know how long we sat like that. But eventually the wind subsided enough for me to see two fir trees standing upright in the ice, perhaps eleven feet apart—one at each end of the open water.

Of course. Vernon West had been here. He owned an icehouse in Tonka Bay. Each winter he stocked up on ice he cut from Lake Minnetonka and then sold it to vacationing city folks. He always marked the open places by drilling a hole in the ice and inserting a fir tree. This time, perhaps because of the freak storm, he had placed two trees. But I hadn't seen either of them because of the blizzard.

How had the dog known? He stopped me in time. If I had continued, I would have plunged into thirty feet of frigid Lake Minnetonka. I owed my life to a little white dog with wise eyes.

"If you come home with me you'll never be hungry again," I told the dog. "You'll have a home with my family forever."

He touched his nose to my cheek. I flinched. My cheek tingled, almost stung.

I looked toward home. I could see the island plainly. Aside from occasional gusts, the storm ended as abruptly as it had begun. Cautiously, the dog and I skirted the open water and headed for our bay. A thread of smoke rose from the chimney of my brother's fish house. When we arrived I pushed open the door. The potbelly stove was still hot, but again I'd missed my brother.

I sat on the bench to catch my breath.

"Here, boy," I called. The dog poked his head in the door and gave me one long, intent look, then backed out. I followed.

"Wait. Come back, dog, stay with me." I called to him again and again.

He'd appeared out of nowhere, and now he'd vanished. I searched all around and tracked my own boot prints in the fresh snow. I found no dog—and no paw prints.

⛧⛧⛧⛧⛧⛧

I didn't think much about that event until forty years later.

I was lying in a hospital bed at Saint Mary's, awaiting a test to show my cardiologist the precise location of a massive artery blockage. I shivered. Fear buffeted me like winter's worst blizzard, chilling me to my core and blinding me from any light of hope.

My thoughts wandered to the time I'd made it across the ice when a skinny white terrier saved my life. That dog. I could almost feel the tingling of my cheek where his nose had touched. What had he been? I'd never thought about it before. A real dog that God used, or a q messenger—an angel—in disguise? No matter. I knew it was God who kept me safe.

As a child I hadn't known about God. But since I'd become a believer, I prayed for others daily and taught my daughters that the Lord is powerful enough to do anything. I knew I should pray now. *Our Father, who art in heaven, hallowed be thy name. Thy kingdom come, thy will . . .*

I couldn't say it. I wanted *my* will to be done. I had lived most of my life making my own way, independent. But now I felt as though I stood on ice with open water close by. I couldn't see where to step safely. I sensed the Lord asking me to release my life into His control.

"I can't!"

There is no other way.

"I want my way."

I am the way. I am truth and life. Trust me.

I inched back in my spirit. *Thy kingdom come, thy will— thy will be done, on earth as it is in heaven. There. Take all of me. My life is yours.*

With those words, warmth poured into me as if the Lord himself had put His arms around my trembling body. I slept in peace.

The next morning my cardio team performed the procedure. At the end of it, the cardiologist looked puzzled.

He shook his head. "The blockage is gone. There is nothing wrong with you. I think we have seen a miracle."

††††††

It doesn't matter if I can't see my destination. I can trust my Father God. I can walk by faith and not by sight, and I won't have to fear stepping into open water.

Angel on Route 495

SUSAN A. J. LYTTEK

L ooks like a storm coming," Matt said, gazing at the sky.
I agreed. "Makes me wish you had driven instead
of me."

"We went over that this morning. Your car gets better gas
mileage than my truck. Also, Gary keeps it a lot neater."

I had to give Matt points for that one. My darling husband never could tolerate mess in his cars. It did make for
neater places for passengers to sit and relax. I knew why I
was driving, but still I wished Matt could take over. I asked
him if he could.

"You know I don't drive stick," he reminded me.

I sighed and started the vehicle. My friend Matt and I had
gone to an all-day Christian writers' workshop in Annapolis,
Maryland, which was a couple hours north from where we

lived. That morning I had picked him up from our church and driven us to the conference. We enjoyed the fellowship and different learning opportunities. But as we left the gathering, the late winter sky looked prematurely dark.

The first major road we hit out of Annapolis was Highway 50. There, traffic ran slow and heavy, part Saturday night, part weather. Before long the rain began.

I turned on the intermittent wipers, then the first setting. But that only lasted until we hit the beltway surrounding Washington, D.C. Traffic-packed and treacherous in the best of circumstances, the 495 loop obviously also had out-of-towners heading south to 95. The rain and impending storm caused mixed reactions from the drivers. Some acted as if the pavement remained dry and drove like they were on a racetrack. Others appeared to equate the rainwater to an inch of fresh snow as they crept along ten to fifteen miles below the speed limit.

I'd lived in the area long enough to recognize the ingredients of an impending highway disaster.

"Don't worry. It'll be fine," Matt said.

But a grimace remained plastered on my face. Matt kept trying to find some words to loosen my death grip on the steering wheel. As a young, single guy, he obviously felt uncomfortable trying to calm this frantic woman.

"Didn't you tell me that you felt the presence of God at today's workshop?"

"Well, yeah."

"I could be wrong, but you said you had fresh direction of where God wanted you to go with your writing ministry. The speaker gave you a lot of ideas on how to better serve God, you said. Do you think God would confirm all that with you and then just take you to Him?"

Cars wove between the lanes in an elaborate dance—with a sprinkling of semis thrown in. I felt like a shuttle weaving through a tangled loom.

"Did you hear me?" Matt asked.

"Yes," I snapped.

"But do you believe it?"

I didn't. Not really. I knew God could protect me and had on many occasions. But why would He want to bother with traffic? Wasn't that my job?

Sensing either that I wasn't comfortable answering that question, or that I wouldn't respond, Matt changed the subject and started talking about a mutual friend who'd moved away from our church and was returning to visit the next week.

I barely heard his prattle, though. I increasingly focused on the vehicles around us and the worsening weather. I paid only minimal attention to him, nodding when I felt a pause in his words warranted it.

As we rounded a curve, I saw a disabled vehicle on the right shoulder about a half mile in front of me. I felt sorry for the driver. Being stranded on this stretch was bad enough, but in this weather? I breathed a quick prayer on her behalf.

However, I didn't feel as sorry as another driver who began cutting across three lanes of traffic to rescue her.

The combination of heavy traffic and bad weather made his maneuver more dangerous than normal. Cars in front of me and to my left slammed on their brakes to avoid hitting the Good Samaritan. Car after car screeched to a halt.

I slammed on my brakes and slid to a stop—only inches from the vehicle in front of me.

Grateful that I hadn't plowed into the car, I took a deep breath. Then I looked in my rearview mirror. I wished I hadn't. Coming behind me, at highway speed, was a pickup that hadn't noticed the commotion.

"Oh, dear God!" I cried, as much of a prayer as a plea.

Matt turned his head to face my terror. Then we both braced for the inevitable crash.

As I watched our doom approach, the impossible happened. A large glowing being, at least twelve to fifteen feet tall, appeared between my little car and the truck. Through its ethereal glow I could still see the truck speeding toward my rear bumper. The being, its back toward me, spread out its arms and formed a barrier. I never saw the truck slow, but still it never hit us. The being's presence stopped it.

"An angel," I breathed, amazed.

As soon as I said it, I could no longer see him. But I knew God had sent an angel to protect us. He had protected me!

Fear evaporated, and nothing—not the weather, not my end-of-the-day exhaustion, not the crazy drivers who surrounded me—could stop me from smiling.

Matt hadn't seen the angel because he had turned around to face the front when he braced himself. But I think after listening to a half hour of my happy confessions until we returned to his vehicle, he believed that I had.

Two things he knew without a doubt. Before our sudden stop, I had been afraid and agitated. Afterward, I became happy and confident in the presence of God.

To him, that was proof enough that something amazing had happened.

But as for me, I know what I saw. My heavenly Father sent an angel to protect me and to prove that even traffic is His job.

Give God Time

JAMES STUART BELL

I was your typical "starving student," and my wife, Margaret, sold fur coats on commission for her aunt in the posh part of Dublin, Ireland, to support us.

Some weeks we'd get minimum wages (no fur sales) and could barely put food on the table. But with the sale of a single coat we would celebrate with a dinner out. We were newly married, and God was putting us in the boot camp of learning trust and dependence on Him to provide for our present and future needs.

We had already learned something of His miraculous provision while in Ireland that academic year. Before returning to the States, however, we very much wanted to visit a particularly beautiful spot in Europe.

I had seen a *National Geographic* cover on my parents' coffee table before we were married, and I had exclaimed, "Let's go there for our honeymoon!" It was a picture of a steepled church on a little island in the middle of ice-blue Lake Bled in the Yugoslavian Alps, with a huge cliff in the background and a castle in the distance.

But when we arrived at our first stop in London after getting married, we had one problem after another and simply couldn't get to Yugoslavia. I told the friend we were staying with in London that we had blown our chance. I would now have to go to Ireland for the semester, our money would run out, and we would have to return to the States and get down to the business of making money and supporting our soon-to-be first baby, daughter Rosheen. Our chance to see the dreamland Alps was slipping away. But our friend said to have faith. She strongly felt we would get there before returning to the States.

The months of studying the genius of the Irish poets, C. S. Lewis, and others flew by, and our vacation period before the trip home was dawning. Sure enough, our meager savings had dwindled and I reminded Margaret of my earlier prediction. But she reminded me of our London friend's faith-filled words that we would make it anyway.

"Give God time," our friend had said. So we watched and waited.

Out of the blue, Margaret's mother let us know she had forgotten to give us a wedding present and sent us two hundred Irish pounds. I said that would get us as far as a round trip to see Margaret's sister Mona in Paris. Then Mona remembered that she had also forgotten to give us anything at our wedding. So she sprung for an additional two hundred quid, as they say over there. That meant we could take the famous Orient Express train all the way through Italy to our destination in Yugoslavia.

It was a wonderful but tightly budgeted vacation. We had those oversized orange backpacks of the '70s and stayed in cut-rate hostels. We ate cheap sandwiches but thrived on romance.

When we returned to Ireland on the train from Europe, we had a paucity of pounds to our name. But I wasn't concerned because we were going to leave for the States shortly and our airline tickets were paid for. We planned to live with my parents for a while as I sought a job in Christian publishing.

But the straightforward plan wasn't meant to be. I was married to an Irish citizen who was planning to settle in the States. As we stood in line at the airport, I wondered how it might be different for her as a foreigner planning on staying in the States permanently.

I found out soon enough. It was an early Sunday morning and we had plenty of time before our flight to Newark, New Jersey. The person at the check-in counter told us that Margaret needed a visa to enter the United States and that we could secure one at the U.S. Embassy. She raced out and grabbed a cab, heading back into a largely deserted Dublin, only to find that no one was available at the embassy on an early Sunday morning.

When she returned to the check-in at the airport, the attendant had more bad news. The next available flight with open seats on Aer Lingus would not be for five days, *and* the fare would go up—for both of us it would cost an additional fifty-five Irish pounds.

We had barely enough money for a cab back to her sister's apartment, where we had been staying. Later that day we sat in the apartment and considered our options.

We could phone Margaret's mother in nearby County Wicklow and borrow the money, or we could borrow from one of our friends. But as we prayed about it, we felt the Lord say that would not be a good witness to the life of faith we espoused.

We had only five days and a few pence to rub together. This was a nail-biter, especially because we had decided to really go out on a limb and prove God by not asking anyone for the funds. Meanwhile, we secured the necessary papers at the American embassy.

A couple days later we received a call from a sweet widow who had been in our Dublin prayer fellowship. Auntie Elsie was like our personal Irish fairy godmother, a wisp of a quiet and lovely woman who was deeply spiritual and heard from the Lord as if He were her best friend. She had not been aware of our departure date and was simply inviting us over to her home for tea.

"Well, at least it's a free meal, although now I'm beginning to feel like a sponge," I told my wife.

When we arrived, Auntie Elsie was as sweet as ever and had a delicious spread of tea, scones, clotted cream, and thick jam awaiting us. We kept mum about our financial need and vaguely told her we planned to return to the States soon.

As we headed for the door with our regretful farewells, she directed us toward a little table with an envelope. It had "Isaiah 55" written on it. Inside were verses one and two: "Is anyone thirsty? Come and drink—even if you have no money! Come, take your choice of wine or milk—it's all free! Why spend your money on food that does not give you strength? Why pay for food that does you no good? Listen to me, and you will eat what is good. You will enjoy the finest food."

My eyes nearly popped out as I noticed what was next to the verses in the envelope—fifty-five Irish pounds, the exact amount we needed!

Auntie Elsie casually added that this was the verse the Lord had given her for us to speed us on our way, and He wanted us to have the equivalent amount of cash as the Isaiah chapter number to go with it.

We were dumbfounded at God's generosity and creativity based on our willingness to take a tiny step of faith by keeping our need secret. We were indeed delighting in the richest of fare, the understanding of His infinite knowledge of every aspect of our lives, big and small, and His ample provision to meet our every need in the future.

Later, a few days after returning to the States, we wandered into our favorite Logos bookstore for some inspirational literature to begin our new life as I sought to be immersed in the workforce, supporting wife and baby Ro.

As Margaret talked to a friend at the counter, I dallied by a spinner-rack of posters. And once again my eyes nearly popped out of my head. There before me was a poster with a photo of the same scene from the *National Geographic* cover—Lake Bled in Yugoslavia, the place I had nearly despaired of going until my London friend said God had told her to give Him time and we would eventually get there if we only continued to believe.

What was even more mind-boggling was the caption on the poster. Why would this particular poster of an obscure place in Yugoslavia be here in Plainfield, New Jersey? Because the poster was meant for Margaret and me. The banner across the lower right corner of the Lake Bled scene read: *Give God Time.*

Whether it was the five days of waiting for the fifty-five pounds to fly back to America, or the five months it took between our wedding day and our honeymoon trip to Lake Bled, God was telling us loud and clear to give Him time to perform His miracles of provision.

Waiting on God can be trying, even frustrating, but it can renew our faith and bear fruit if we trust in a faithful God.

Bear Hugs in Heaven

G. L. FRANCIS

Hannah died a month before her twentieth birthday. As my youngest sister's daughter, she was my niece. But because my sister couldn't care for her, our parents had adopted Hannah, so she was my sister as well as my niece.

The situation tickled her sense of humor. "My Papa is my dad, and my Nanny is my mom," she recited at school when asked to tell about her family. "My mother is my sister, and my aunts are my sisters."

We were as close as sisters separated by decades could be, sharing our love of horses and dogs, arts and crafts, rocks and ramen noodles. Her dyslexia made reading a challenge, but she loved listening to stories read to her. She planned our annual day at the local Renaissance festival several months in advance: what shows we would see, what trinkets we would buy, which food kiosks we would try.

In her more somber moments, Hannah told me that kids in her class teased her about being raised by grand-parents. She worried privately about how old our parents were, about what would happen if they died before she finished school.

"No fear," I told her. "You'll have a home with us if any-thing like that happens."

My husband and I had often discussed the probability of providing for her and finishing her upbringing when my parents—neither in good health—became too infirm.

She gave me a fierce, rib-compressing bear hug, then grinned.

"So, then I'll have to say that my Nanny is my mom, my mother is my sister, and my aunt is my sister and my mom."

We burst into gales of laughter.

Occasionally, I'd get an urgent call from her.

"Nanny's been reading the book of James to me again." Exasperation oozed from Hannah's young voice.

Ah, yes. James. Chapter and applicable verse. We all grew up hearing James every time Mom thought the situation required it. "Were you acting snobby or sassy?"

Mumble, mumble.

I snickered. "Sorry, I can't hear you."

"Sassy. She said I couldn't wear my riding boots to church. I told her if I couldn't, I wasn't going."

At age fifteen, a wreck changed Hannah's life. The pickup she was in rolled and threw her through the back window. The driver walked away and left her lying in the ditch, her back broken and hips fractured. Someone passing by found her hours later.

Doctors told Hannah she'd never walk, but she'd grown up watching family members battle devastating health problems. Stubborn streaks are genetic. She shed no tears. Her eyes narrowed and jaw tightened. "Yes, I will," she announced.

Though her back and hips healed permanently crooked, she was walking within a few months. Within a year, she was riding again. She and our folks moved farther away to a little farm where she finally got a horse of her own.

Four years passed. Although she was in constant pain from the wreck, Hannah improved her riding skills and began working toward competition riding.

She bought a Shetland sheepdog and studied canine training, showing, and breeding. She dreamed of developing a line of show shelties that could work equally well with sheepherding duties. She worked part-time as a kennel person and occasional assistant in a veterinary clinic, saving toward the stable and kennel she hoped to build one day.

Hannah participated in church activities and helped with children in special needs ministry, becoming famous (and infamous) for her joyful bear hugs. She collected stuffed animals—unicorns, horses, dogs. She never quit, never gave up.

Then one day Dad called me at work with his voice quavering. "She's dead."

At first I thought he was talking about Mom. Her health had steadily declined over the last several months. Then I understood—he meant Hannah.

There's no way to rehearse for anything like this. The news tackled my guts, and none of the oxygen on earth could find a way into my lungs. Long seconds stretched into eternity before I could ask what happened.

Three days before, something in her car's steering had failed and she'd lost control. Her car had gone off a bridge and plunged into the icy river, swollen and swift with February thaw. Immediately, drivers behind her had stopped to give aid. Call it luck or call it divine providence, but the first person was an EMT on his way to work, and the second was an emergency room nurse just off shift.

Hannah had managed to get free of the submerged car and made it to a narrow ledge a dozen feet below the highway shoulder before she collapsed from severe hypothermia. Other drivers lowered the two medically trained rescuers down to her.

She'd spent the night in the hospital. Her body's core temperature rose from a perilous 71.4 to 97 degrees. Although she'd suffered no broken bones and only a few minor scrapes and bruises, the hypothermia worsened her pain from the previous wreck.

In spite of swallowing and inhaling icy river water, she seemed well enough to be released the next day. She went home, but she couldn't remember anything after the car went underwater. She didn't know how she got out or how she made it to that narrow ledge.

"On my way, Dad."

I could only think of how tears of laughter rolled down Hannah's cheeks every time she was happy, and the bear hugs she gave every time I gave her any little gift—even just a pretty rock I'd found. It seemed out of order, losing a person still in her teens.

Even strong faith asks *why?* however briefly, when the unthinkable happens. God doesn't answer in a great booming voice from behind billowing clouds outlined with a corona of sunbeams. His answers come subtly, indirectly. Sometimes they whisper in the monotonous sound of tires on pavement while you're driving to prepare for a funeral. They appear in seeing the cane, the braces, the additional medicines no longer needed. They're in the somber gazes of two sheepdogs who stayed by a young girl's side to the very end.

Sometimes answers begin arriving in nearly identical calls from strangers who stopped to help her.

"I was so sorry to hear about Hannah."

"Thank you. I'll pass it on to my family. They'll appreciate it." It was my turn to field phone calls, relieving Mom and Dad if only for a little while.

"I . . . ummm . . . I wanted to tell you something about that day at the river. But please don't think I'm crazy. It was just too strange not to let you know."

I closed my eyes and took a deep breath. I really didn't want to hear some nut case gabble on about the accident. But courtesy overrode my urge to hang up on the caller. "Many strange things happen in life. Just because we can't explain them doesn't mean we're crazy."

The person on the line hesitated.

"There was someone already on that ledge helping Hannah when we got there. Impossible, I know. No way he could've gotten there without being seen. And the ledge was only a few yards long. There wasn't any approach from the bank."

I frowned at the phone. Hannah had been alone in the car. Hadn't she?

"But he wasn't there when they brought her and the other two up from the ledge." Another hesitation, then the caller added, "And his clothes were dry, even though splashes from the river soaked the two we lowered within minutes."

The nurse who'd been on the ledge with Hannah called. She said much the same as the other caller, but with additional details.

"The air felt weird—calm even though there was a stout breeze. Made my skin and bones feel like they were humming. And that guy—we were so busy with Hannah, I didn't get a good look at his face, but he had on jeans and a brown flannel shirt. Absolutely dry. He stepped aside when the men dropped me down to the ledge."

The EMT told us, "There was some guy in a brown flannel shirt down there. Didn't say anything. I was wrapping my coat around your sister, and I glanced up to ask if he was okay. He was gone. And no one on the shoulder helped him up from there. . . . Dude was bone dry, but we were drenched to the skin just from river spray."

Another person who'd helped from atop the highway's shoulder said, "I got no clue what happened. I tell ya, my bones still tingle just thinkin' about how the air felt. I was gonna toss my roofing harness down to help 'em bring her up. I swear there were four people, including your sister, on that ledge. I looked away for a second when the ambulance arrived, but when I looked back, there were only three."

And then, the same wondering question from each caller. "Do you think maybe an angel helped her that day?"

But why? It made no sense. If it was her time to die, why the rescue?

On the back porch of our parents' home, I sat brushing the silky, thick coat of Hannah's oldest dog when the rest of the quiet answers came.

There was something the individuals who'd helped her needed to see that day. Maybe those few simply but desperately needed a divine encounter.

Hannah's death was a deliverance from the rapidly accelerating deterioration of her internal organs resulting from the first wreck. But, for whatever unknowable reason there might be, she was never meant to die in the icy river, alone and afraid. She passed quietly in her sleep, with people who loved her nearby, with her beloved dogs beside her bed and her horse in the pasture beyond her window, and with her favorite things surrounding her.

Hannah's passing left a hole in our lives, but God consoled us with blessings of comfort and assurance that we would be reunited in time.

As I hugged her dog, unbidden images flashed in my heart.

Hannah having serious words with James about those "control your tongue" verses he wrote so long ago.

Hannah pestering Jesus to let her ride the horses of the angelic cavalry who would accompany Him in the last days.

Hannah passing out joyful bear hugs in heaven.

Getting the Blob off My Bed

◆———◆

INGRID SHELTON

I t can't be true, yet it has to be," I mumbled as I read
Charles Darwin's theory of evolution.

It seemed so logical and made perfect sense that life
as we know it had evolved from one single organism or bit
of matter.

Was I deceived to believe God created the earth? I wondered.

My weak faith began to disintegrate as I continued reading page after page.

As a graduate student, I was to evaluate evolution and creation and discuss which theory could be trusted most. After
reading the next few pages, I became convinced that creation
was a figment of the imagination. And I was glad to finally
be enlightened as to the origin of the species. What seemed
to me to be compelling evidence for evolution caused me to

immediately join the ranks of confirmed atheists. Disregarding my former belief in a God who created the universe didn't particularly affect me since my relationship with God had been on shaky ground.

I talked to some other students about creation and evolution.

"It really doesn't matter what you believe. Both are just theories, as far as I can determine," one classmate said with a shrug.

"Just choose one theory that appeals to you and that you can defend best," another responded.

"Read the Bible for yourself and then arrive at a conclusion," still another student advised.

Yet reading the Bible didn't particularly interest me. I had skimmed through several books of the New Testament in the past, but the truth contained therein hadn't sunk into my mind or heart. Furthermore, I prayed only when I wanted something from God; now I didn't need to pray to a God who I believed was nonexistent.

A few months after my declaration for atheism, as I was drifting off to sleep, I was shocked to see a large blob sitting at the foot of my bed. Instinctively I knew this blob was a demon that had come to devour me. It looked like a large, misshapen ball with some sort of head at the top and small holes for eyes.

I bolted upright in fright and anger.

"Get away!" I screamed. The blob inched toward me.

"Get off!" I screamed again, ready to fight. With fists outstretched, I delivered my first blow, but it bounced right back, not leaving a mark. I knew I had to get the thing off my bed. My life depended on it.

Again and again I struck it with all my strength, determined not to let it come any closer, yet each blow bounced off that menacing blob like a rubber ball off a brick wall. I lost track of time as I punched that demon with my fists, delivering blow after blow. Yet no matter how hard I punched, I couldn't get the blob off my bed.

Panic filled my heart as I realized I was no match for this evil one. Yet I had to succeed. I couldn't and wouldn't let it devour me.

My heart beat like a hammer. My fear escalated.

The demon inched closer even though I delivered my blows like a machine gun, using all my strength to ward off the inevitable. Then a widening grin appeared on that blob's head.

"No!" I screamed at the demon as I continued to deliver blow after blow. Horrified, I realized I had lost the battle.

But I remembered, "The Spirit who lives in you is greater than the spirit who lives in the world" (1 John 4:4).

"Jesus!" I cried. As soon as I mentioned the name of Jesus, the demon disappeared. Instantly! Gone just like that!

Now wide awake, I was still sitting upright in bed, trembling and drenched in sweat, with fists outstretched, ready to deliver further blows.

But I was alone.

Relieved and exhausted, I sank down on my pillow. My mind churned. I knew I had actually been trying to fight the Evil One physically. I couldn't have just dreamed it. My heart was still hammering, my body was soaked in sweat, and my outstretched arms with fists ready to deliver more blows were proof I couldn't ignore.

Then another thought occurred to me: If the devil was real, then what about God? Hadn't He just delivered me from the Evil One when I called on Him?

The implications of what I had just experienced shattered my belief system. If there was a God, then the theory of evolution was just that—a theory that could not be scientifically proven as true. But could I trust the creation story as stated in the Bible? I knew I must. I now had proof that the spiritual world existed. The more I thought about it, the more I became convinced that the whole idea of evolution was preposterous. I was now determined to trust the creation story and the God who had created heaven and earth as stated in the Bible.

As I began to read the New Testament, I slowly became convinced of the truth of the Bible. Eventually I came across 1 Peter 5:8: "Stay alert! Watch out for your great enemy, the devil. He prowls around like a roaring lion, looking for someone to devour."

"Yes," I murmured. "How true!"

I had struggled against the spiritual forces of evil, and only by calling on the name of Jesus had victory come.

And when I read Ephesians 6:11, "Put on all of God's armor so that you will be able to stand firm against all strategies of the devil," I realized that I needed to learn to do just that.

But most of all, I learned that there is power in the name of Jesus. Jesus won the victory over death on the cross and grants power to overcome the Evil One to all those who call on His name, to those who trust in His name. Clearly, God had shown me that Jesus is the only weapon we need to overcome the powers of darkness.

Wings of Peace

CHERYL CHRISTENSEN JOHNSTON

Pollyanna" is what my husband, R.J., calls me.

Normally I'm an upbeat, see-the-good-in-all-things, blessings overflowing type of person. My childhood home was filled with laughter, and until I was twelve, my father sang encouraging songs to me like "You Are My Sunshine" and "Let the Sunshine In."

But a month after my mother died, depression attacked me.

I was aware of my mother's faith from my earliest memories. Her parents were evangelists, and the Michigan church they established is now more than eighty years old. Five of their seven children became preachers.

When my mom was fourteen, her world shattered when her beloved mother died. Desperation triggered knee-jerk decisions that took her to California, away from family and faith, and into two divorces by the age of nineteen. She longed for someone to fill the hole in her heart.

The next year my mother, Dorcas Roberta Spooner, married Robert Vernon Christensen, and they vowed "until death do us part."

Five years later I was born, and by my parents' seventh anniversary, along came the twins, Peggy and Paula. Like all young families, ours juggled finances, but overall, life was good and we were happy . . . that is until diabetes took Daddy from us when he was only forty-two years old.

At his funeral, I remember seeing my strong, independent thirty-seven-year-old mother crumble. I watched her sink into despair, afraid of our future.

Many mornings Paula, Peggy, and I would awaken to discover our mother had fallen asleep with an open Bible across her chest. And many nights we saw her on her knees, praying.

For the rest of her life she relied on God.

Mom always loved holidays, especially Christmas. She tried to make things special for her three daughters, with touches like trinket-filled stockings, new pajamas with slipper socks, the traditional turkey dinner, and several extra special presents she somehow found the money to purchase.

Mom enjoyed driving us through neighborhoods to see lighted Christmas displays. We also attended Christmas productions at nearby churches. And in the house where she lived alone in her later years, she played piano and sang Christmas carols just for her own and God's enjoyment.

Seven days before Mom's death at age seventy in 1995, our extended family shared a beautiful but bittersweet Thanksgiving. Everyone gathered at Paula's house to share the turkey dinner, family games, and conversations. By evening Mom was struggling to smile. The lung cancer she'd battled the previous year had invaded her stomach and brain. On this night it had sapped her stamina, and dark circles underlined her eyes.

We certainly didn't suspect that within the week Jesus would welcome her home.

In the weeks after her funeral, I didn't want to dress or eat or even step outside. I had no interest in celebrating Christmas. We had no gift-wrapped packages or decorated tree or anything to make our home holiday ready.

Sitting alone in the dark house on December 22, I couldn't shake the grief and depression that overwhelmed me. Sobbing uncontrollably, I called a dear friend for help. When she heard the anguish in my voice, she began to pray. She begged God to calm my spirit and comfort me, to cover and enfold me. She asked that I would feel His love and presence in a palpable way.

Her prayer worked.

Even though my heart wasn't in it, by day's end I had managed to purchase and wrap gifts for R.J., our grandbabies, our sons, and their wives.

By ten that evening, I was relaxed but exhausted when I fell into bed, my eyes still swollen from tears. Thoughts and sweet memories of my mother cradled my deep sleep.

Suddenly I was awake, still on my back with eyes open wide. On the dresser to the right, the digital alarm clock read 2:45.

I heard a noise and looked toward the sliding glass door on the room's western wall.

A large white bird perched on the valance rod above the door.

Thinking my eyes were playing tricks on me, I used thumbs and forefingers to pry them open even more.

Sure enough, there was a white bird—posed, as if on a mission.

With one quick swoosh of its wings, it swooped down and hovered over the bed, startling me. My arms flailed as I clutched the sheets and tried to wake R.J.

The bird's wings sounded like rushing, whispered wind.

My chest heaved—not in fear, but in awe.

The bird pronounced one word, slowly and with authority. "Peace!"

As the wings fluttered gracefully, the bird spoke again. "Peace! This is for Cheryl. Your mother is in heaven."

My heart leaped inside my chest as I panted for breath.

I remember realizing the bird was actually a dove.

I remember understanding this message was meant only for me.

I remember staring, amazed at the experience.

And I remember feeling infinitely loved as I drifted back into sleep.

When I awoke later that morning from one of my best rests ever, R.J. asked, "What went on in here last night?"

I started to explain, but his laughter sealed my lips.

But I know.

And whether or not anyone else believes what I saw, I know.

The dove's words offered an assurance that changed my life—the peace that forever passes all understanding.

The Total Package

JEANIE JACOBSON

In May 1989, while I was on my way to pick up my daughter from kindergarten, a school bus rear-ended and totaled my 1968 Galaxy 500. Because I was strapped in by the car's only safety feature—a lap belt—the impact severely wrenched my spine.

The accident left me suffering with intense pain in my neck and back. Every movement was agony. When I took the medications the doctors prescribed, I slept. Without the medications, the pain was unbearable.

After the accident, my husband, Jake, took on the role of family caregiver. After his night job as a press operator, he'd come home to make breakfast, get our five-year-old daughter, Patty, ready for school, take care of the pets, clean the house, and take me to medical appointments.

"I'm sorry you're stuck doing all the work," I'd apologize. Jake would stroke my hair and reassure me. "I love you. Just rest and get better. I'll take care of everything."

Jake did a marvelous job, but Patty missed having an active and attentive mother. Every day she asked the same questions: "Are you better today, Mommy?" "Mommy, will you play with me?" "Mommy, why can't we go to the playground?"

Every day I disappointed her with the same answer: "I'm sorry, sweetie. Mommy's not better yet."

Her dejected look tore my heart as she'd pat my arm and say, "It's okay, Mommy. I still love you."

As the weeks wore on my husband wore down. The long hours at his job, the cooking, cleaning, laundry, pet care, yard work, and caring for our daughter and me had taken its toll. He was lucky to get a few hours of rest a day, while I spent most of my days in a drugged sleep.

I felt useless, was often bedridden, and was always guilt ridden. I wept the day I overheard our daughter ask, "Daddy, when will Mommy be better?"

Jake paused before he answered wearily, "Honey, I wish I knew."

Weeks rolled into months. Despite repeated doctor visits, I wasn't improving.

Hopelessness overwhelmed us the day Jake and I sat in the neurologist's office and heard his prognosis. Medically, there was no help for me. The neurologist explained that the pain might eventually lessen but warned us that my condition might never improve.

From that day we spiraled into a dark pit. Our marriage began to fracture. My once loving husband, overworked and overburdened, withdrew from me. Jake and I separated, and he filed for divorce.

My neighbor, Kris, had been active in our lives from the time of the accident to offer help and prayer. I wanted the help but wasn't interested in the prayer. Her conversations about Jesus made me uncomfortable, especially since Kris acted like He was her best friend.

One Sunday afternoon in October Kris phoned and told me, "A missionary is speaking at our church tonight. The Lord said you need to be there."

Jake and I had always declined Kris's church invitations. That day, unable to care for my daughter, my marriage falling apart, my body and soul in anguish, I finally said yes to Kris.

That evening her church family welcomed me, but I was on edge. Voices in my head urged, *Get out of here. These people are crazy. They just want your money. Get out before you get sucked in.*

As I stood to leave, the missionary, a small, unassuming man, walked to the microphone.

Get out, get out, get out! those voices screamed. But I couldn't move.

The missionary bowed his head for a moment, then spoke with a voice of absolute authority, "Satan, I bind you and all your demons in the name of Jesus and command you to be still."

Instantly the voices in my head stopped shrieking.

I listened while the missionary explained how Jesus had died on the cross for our sins. When he finished he said, "If you want Jesus in your life, come forward."

With Kris beside me, I hurried to the altar to pray, "Jesus, please forgive my sins and be my Savior."

At that moment I met the living God. His love and peace washed over me. Joy replaced the darkness trapping me. The demonic voices that I'd mistaken for my own thoughts were silenced. I was free.

Kris hugged me and said, "Salvation is a total package. Jesus will heal your body if you ask Him to."

Love, peace, joy, and healing, too? Oh yes, I wanted that!

Kris explained my situation to the missionary. He laid his hand on my head to pray, but tremors racked my body. I collapsed onto the floor, shaking and writhing. Demonic voices, now outside my head rather than inside it, screeched a cacophony of indistinguishable sounds.

"I've never seen the Holy Spirit manifest himself like this," Kris said.

"That's not the Holy Spirit," the missionary answered. He stretched his hand over me and commanded, "Satan, leave her alone. She belongs to Jesus."

My muscles immediately relaxed. I felt as if I were cradled in God's arms. For a long time I simply rested in His presence.

When I was ready, Kris helped me stand. I realized the pain that had held me captive was gone. Gingerly at first, then with more abandon, I craned my neck, stretched my back, touched my toes, and even jumped up and down. All pain free.

Overcome with gratitude, I sank to my knees, hands raised in thanksgiving and praise to the God who had saved me, delivered me from the powers of darkness, and healed me.

In the following months, the Lord continued to pour out gifts from His "total salvation package," including restoration. God healed our marriage and mended our family.

More than two decades have passed since then, and we rejoice more than ever in God's total salvation package.

No Longer Abandoned

JUDY HAMPTON

T he church is hosting a marriage enrichment seminar next month. It's only a day and a half long. Would you like to go?" I asked my husband, Orvy, timidly, knowing he'd probably pass on it.

"Sure!" he exclaimed.

I was shocked. Only two years had passed since we'd been in the middle of a total marriage meltdown. Divorce had seemed imminent.

Actually, life had been tough from the day we married.

I'd met my football-hero husband in high school. It was love at first sight. We married shortly after graduation, which was not that unusual for our era. Plus, I was pregnant when we got married, which also was not unusual for our era.

Orvy went to college on a football scholarship, and I gave up college to work as a secretary and support our goal: his college degree. At night we juggled four part-time jobs.

Our life was hard, with periods of intense misery. We barely made ends meet and often went hungry. We had to save money to pay for the doctor and the hospital for when our baby was born.

Several months after our dismal wedding, our son entered the world. It was instant love, but this new responsibility added more financial burden, which stretched our patience and bank account to the breaking point.

Finances, or the lack of them, consumed me. I longed for security of some kind. Add to this my immaturity, selfishness, and envy of friends whose parents helped them financially. As a result, I was a contentious woman with unfulfilled expectations.

With each year our marriage declined until I wanted to be anywhere but home. Our only hope was Orvy's getting out of college with a degree so we could capture the American dream. But right before his graduation, my world fell apart. I came home after work and found a letter propped up on the kitchen table: "Judy, I have to get away and find myself. I don't know what I want to do with my life since I didn't receive a pro football contract. I'm sorry."

I slumped into a chair. I'd been abandoned . . . *again*. Two days later I found out I was pregnant *again*.

For the second time in my life I begged God to let me die.

Abandonment had actually been a backdrop for my whole life. From an early age I was worried sick because Daddy was always out of work. I didn't understand that his unemployment was because of his alcohol problem. Mom hid his problems, just as she hid her own alcohol abuse.

Still, I was ambitious and determined to make something of myself. When I was twelve years old I began cleaning houses with my best friend. I worked after school and weekends so I could buy cute clothes and shoes like my friends had. I was devastated when my mom insisted I share that money with her. A dutiful child of alcoholic parents, I gave her my checks.

I was trained from a very young age to enable and feel sorry for my parents. I lived in a lot of fear because I knew they were not interested in physically taking care of me.

I questioned why none of my friends ever had to worry about money, why they didn't have to work to buy school clothes.

I felt emotionally abandoned, as well. Even though I was popular in high school—a cheerleader, in the royal court, a student leader—my parents never came to any events to support me or even cared what I did.

The first time I asked God to let me die was when I was still in high school. Because of the situation in our home, I not only felt abandoned by my parents, but I also felt betrayed. Since I couldn't trust my parents, I didn't really trust anyone.

On the day of my graduation Daddy had left a suicide note and disappeared. Mom simply bailed emotionally. She had grown up with wealth and privilege and her life had come to this. She felt it was beneath her to have to work. So my brother and I had to handle the practical sides of life. Devastated and gripped with terror, I fell into the arms of my boyfriend.

I thought I'd never see my dad again. But one day he just showed up. He didn't apologize for the trauma and never addressed his alcoholism.

Fear became my constant companion: fear of his leaving again, fear of poverty, and fear of failure. I went to work right after high school for a mortgage company, but once again I was told to hand over my paychecks to help poor Daddy out.

When I learned I was pregnant two months after high school graduation, I had another reason to be paralyzed with fear.

When I finally told my parents, they basically abandoned me *again*. They said I was a disgrace to our family and, "You've made your bed, now sleep in it. You'll get no help from us."

True to their word, they never did help me. I was crushed—especially after all I'd done to help them and take care of them. I fell into a deep depression and I wanted to run away like my dad, but I had no place to go. I gave up all my dreams of college and got married.

When my husband left me four years later, I realized I could never trust another soul.

After Orvy left, I moved home with my parents. A few weeks before our beautiful daughter's birth, my husband begged for forgiveness. He promised he'd spend the rest of his life making up for what he had put me through. Not only did I not believe him, I had little hope of our marriage surviving. But I was desperate so we reconciled.

Orvy got a job that paid well, and we moved into a bigger apartment. We tried desperately to put back the pieces of our shattered life, but each day fresh fear invaded my soul. I was consumed by thoughts of being abandoned again.

We tried to make our marriage work, but we lacked the power within for any long-term change. We were just trying to manage our fallen humanity. After two years of striving, something happened. I got a phone call from a friend who'd stood by me through thick and thin.

"Judy, are you going to be home this afternoon? I'd love to come by and see the kids," Harriet said. I assured her I would be home.

After we exchanged pleasantries, Harriet and I sat down for a cup of coffee, and she asked if she could share something with me. "Sure," I replied.

Harriet pulled out a small Gospel tract called "The Four Spiritual Laws." She began to read the first page. I was overwhelmed at the question, "Do you know that God loves you and has a plan for your life?"

I immediately started to cry. I didn't know whether God loved me or had abandoned me, as well. When Harriet got to the final pages of that tract, I was sobbing. She sweetly asked, "Judy, would you like to pray and receive Christ as your Savior?"

I nodded yes as tears streamed down my cheeks.

Right there in my tiny dining room, while the fall leaves were changing colors outside, Jesus was changing my heart. I wept as I asked Him to forgive me of my sins. I told Him I believed He died for them, and then, joyously, I invited Him into my life. I didn't fully understand the magnitude of my little prayer, but immediately I knew something supernatural had happened to me.

As I waved good-bye to my precious friend, I walked back into the house and saw two beautiful children—children I'd looked at as a liability to my self-driven life. I wrapped my arms around them and kissed them while I silently thanked God for giving these two precious ones to me. They didn't know it then, but Jesus was giving my children a new mommy.

A few hours later Orvy came home from work. He took one look at me and asked, "What's going on? What's happened? You look different."

I told him I'd become a Christian.

"Oh!" he said matter-of-factly. "I did that when I was twelve."

You sure could've fooled me, buddy, I thought, but I said nothing. I knew my life had been changed in a moment.

A few weeks later my husband had an encounter with Jesus Christ and recommitted his life to the Lord. God began to resurrect our dead marriage and set it on higher ground.

Three months after our life change, Orvy was transferred to Texas. There, someone from his office invited us to church.

We told no one about our painful past. We thought people would judge us for having had so many marital problems and having to get married. So we acted as though we were the cookie-cutter Christian family. A few months later we heard about the marriage enrichment seminar.

We arrived at the church on a Friday evening. Everyone was friendly and seemed to have their lives together much more than we did. But as the evening wore on we were astounded by the number of couples who openly talked about their marital problems and how Jesus Christ had changed them.

We looked at each other as if to say, "I thought we were the only people in the free world with problems."

The evening was packed with riveting testimonies about transformed lives and new beginnings. We were spellbound and arrived the next morning with great anticipation. The day passed at warp speed.

"As we close this seminar, we would like to encourage you to go into the sanctuary, one couple at a time, and pray together," the leader instructed. We'd never prayed together in our entire married life.

We headed toward the sanctuary, a bit embarrassed about our prayer-less life. As we sheepishly stepped into the sanctuary, it was empty. A soft light from behind a large wooden cross illuminated the room. At the altar we held hands and awkwardly knelt to pray.

Before we could utter a word, someone came up behind us and nuzzled between us. He put his arms around us and began to pray.

Who is this guy? I wondered.

This stranger began to pray about things we'd never told a soul: our shameful past, our difficult marriage and the years of strife, lost dreams, and separation. He asked God to heal our marriage and encouraged us to seek Him with all our hearts and trust Him to provide all our needs. He prayed that we would put the past behind us and give our future to God.

His voice was so soothing, his words wrapped in so much love. I desperately wanted to turn around and get a glimpse of him, but I was too mesmerized by his presence. Tears flowed down my cheeks, tears of joy I'd never known in my life.

When he was finished, we stood and turned to thank this precious man, but no one was there. We were all alone in the dimly lit sanctuary.

It took some time before we comprehended what had taken place that day. We'd had a visit from an angel of the Lord. To this day we joyfully recall our time with our unexpected visitor.

We are grateful God doesn't consult our past to determine our future. He simply makes all things new. This year we celebrate fifty-two years of marriage.

Who Has Seen the Wind?

BETTY JOHNSON DALRYMPLE

As if in a trance, I walked to the window and watched the sun set over the mountains.

"Honey," I whispered to my daughter, Richelle. "I'm a widow. Can you believe it? Me, the little girl who never liked being alone; the fear-filled mother who often slept on your guest bed when your father traveled." I paused, then added, "He knew about my fears, especially the nightmares, and he always reassured me, but now he's gone."

I cried.

Twelve hours earlier, at 5:30 a.m., the doctor had awakened me with a gentle tap on the shoulder and whispered, "Mrs. Johnson, your husband isn't breathing and he has no heartbeat. Come with me."

Dazed, I let him take my hand and lead me out of the hospital room and settle me in a chair beside the door.

For the previous five nights, I'd slept on a cot in Richard's room, knowing in my mind that our enemy, colon cancer, was winning the battle.

However, in my heart I still didn't believe anybody or any disease could win against my big, healthy, I-can-do-anything husband. After all, we'd known each other since we were first-graders, and we'd been married forty-six years. Even when the man in the green surgeon's outfit had announced four months earlier, "There is no hope. His cancer is metastasized. He has days, maybe weeks, hopefully a few months," I didn't believe there was no hope. How could I?

"We are a family of faith," I'd choked through my sobs. "There is always hope."

"You're not alone, Mom." Richelle jolted me back to the present and reassured me with a hug. "I'll stay the night with you. After everyone leaves we'll make the bed in the guest room. It's been a long day for all of us," she said as she wiped her tears.

Soon our other two children and the close friends who'd spent the day with us began leaving, each one reassuring me they would do all they could to help me. "We'll be here for you," they said.

"Thanks," I mumbled, but inside I rebelled. *I want Richard. He understands my problems with fear and anxiety. He knows he's like a security blanket for me, the person I depend on to keep me safe.*

Now, just my daughter and I stood looking out the window—listening to the deafening sound of silence.

"Mom, you know we're not alone," Richelle tried to reassure me again. "You're the one who's always taught us that

God will never leave us nor forsake us. We've got to cling to that belief now." Then she added, "And I think Dad is still with us in spirit, too."

"Thank you," I said. "We all need to keep reminding each other of those truths."

"Do you want me to sleep with you? Or would you rather I sleep in the guest room?" she asked.

"I feel like I'd rather be alone," I answered. "I know that means I'll be at one end of the house and you'll be at the other, but I just need time to digest some of the day's events and ask God a few of my many 'why' questions."

"I know how you like to have all the doors locked," Richelle said. "You'll rest better if you know we're safely tucked in for the night, so let's go downstairs and check on the sliding glass door."

We went down the steps, put the bar across the window, then came back upstairs and secured the locks on the main floor. When we turned the lock on the door to the deck, I commented, "I'm so glad we never built steps going to the ground from this deck. I always feel safer this way, and I definitely will now that I'm alone."

"Good night, Mom. I love you," my daughter said as she hugged me.

"And I love you," I said. "I'm so glad I have you, and I'm very thankful you're spending the night with me."

Finally, after tossing, turning, and pleading with God for comfort, I cried myself to sleep.

Music, I hear music. I awakened and listened. *It sounds like chimes.*

I sat up. The chimes continued to ring, and I heard noise coming from the kitchen. I tiptoed to the kitchen, and there stood Richelle, eyes wide and gaping at the open door to the deck.

"Can you believe this, Mom? I heard the chimes and opened my bedroom door. I felt wind on my cheek and wondered where it came from," she stammered. "Look, the door is wide open. We locked it, remember? I know we did."

"I . . . I don't know what's happening." I struggled to speak while staring at the door. "What time is it?"

"The clock on the stove says 5:30," she answered.

Slowly, I smiled.

"Twenty-four hours. Your father's been gone one whole day. Do you suppose the Holy Spirit came to check on us and reassure us that Richard's with God now and they're going to keep us safe?"

"Wow, Mom, do you really believe that?"

"Yes, I do," I answered. "I believe we just experienced the wind of the Holy Spirit."

As if that comforting episode wasn't enough to give me the peace and strength I needed to endure the days ahead, God must have known I'd need another reminder of His constant presence.

Two weeks later my eleven-year-old grandson spent the night with me. Before we went to bed, he challenged me to a game of cards. We had a rousing game of hearts, and then I followed my nightly ritual of locking doors and talking to God, tossing and turning, and finally dozing off.

Suddenly, strong gusts of wind shook my bedroom windows and awakened me.

Wow, we must have some bad weather blowing our way, I thought. Since it was wintertime in Colorado, that wasn't unusual.

The next morning when I walked into the kitchen, my grandson sat there staring at the open deck door.

"Look, Nana," he said. "The door is open and our playing cards blew all over the table and floor."

I looked outside. The trees were still. No sign of a storm.

"What's wrong, Nana? Why are you crying?" he asked.

"These are thankful tears," I smiled. "I think maybe God came for a visit to let us know that He and your grandfather are still watching over us," I added.

"Really, Nana?" he responded. "Wow, that's super!"

After he left for school, I needed to confirm my awesome nighttime visitor, so I called my neighbor and asked, "Did you hear the wind gusting during the night? My windows were rattling so loud it woke me up."

"No, I never heard any wind," she said. Then she asked her husband. "No, he didn't hear it, either," she added.

I could hardly wait to make my next phone call.

"Richelle, guess who called on me during the night?" I asked. "Did you hear the wind blowing around five this morning?"

"No, did you?" she asked. I heard the hope in her voice.

When I finished telling her about the open deck door and the playing cards scattered on the floor, she murmured, "Thank you, God, for sending your messenger."

"Yes," I answered. "The wind of the Holy Spirit continues His reassuring visits. He keeps reminding us what the Lord said is true: 'I will never leave you nor forsake you'" (Hebrews 13:5 ESV).

Glowing Red Eyes

Loretta Eidson

I thought glowing red eyes were only visual effects used in horror movies. I never even imagined their being a reality—until I participated in a private prayer session with two ladies.

When I first joined the prayer ministry at my church, I knew I'd connected with a very special group. I was raised in a Christian home, so I was familiar with prayer. However, the intensity with which this group prayed opened my eyes to a whole new level and understanding of prayer.

We often held special times of intercession when people encountered difficult situations. As we prayed for them, sometimes people cried or even laughed. Usually people just appreciated the prayer and went their way.

Occasionally I stood back and listened as others prayed because I was so intrigued by the way they spoke with authority, quoted Scripture, and talked to God as if He were standing right in front of them. I was mesmerized when I realized we could pray that way.

One summer day my prayer partner, Tonya, called to see if I could meet with her and another lady at the church during the lunch hour. I gladly accepted the invitation.

When I arrived at the church I went to the sanctuary, where I began to pray while I waited for the other ladies to arrive. I opened my Bible and prayed through Ephesians 6, which discusses the armor of God.

As I completed my Bible reading, Tonya and a woman in business attire entered the sanctuary.

"Renee, this is my prayer partner, Jean. Jean, this is Renee."

"It's nice to meet you," I said as I shook Renee's cold hand and looked into her heavy eyes.

Renee told us how she'd felt bothered by an unusual heaviness. She said her attitude would change without warning—normally jovial, she'd suddenly be mean to people. She was also having nightmares and had been impatient and restless.

Tears filled her eyes as she told us examples of her behavior. I realized this wouldn't be an easy time of prayer.

Tonya read a few Bible passages before we prayed. I wasn't certain just how Tonya wanted to handle the prayer, so I motioned for her to take the lead. We stood at the front of the sanctuary. Renee faced Tonya while I stood behind her. Tonya took Renee's hands and began praying. I silently asked God to give Renee His peace and to deliver her from any spiritual attacks of the enemy.

We had been praying for about thirty minutes when I heard a hissing sound. I looked around the sanctuary, wondering if the pastor or someone was trying to get our attention. No one was there, so I returned my focus to Renee.

Hsssss.

Tonya's eyes widened. She glanced at me just as Renee fell to the floor on her stomach. I tried to catch her, but she was heavier than I expected. As soon as she hit the floor, she began to wiggle her body with the winding rhythm of a snake. Smooth, flowing movements pushed her inch by inch along the floor.

She lifted her head and hissed. Her tongue jutted in and out and back and forth like a snake's.

Goose bumps crawled from my head to my toes—though strangely, I was never afraid.

I'd read in the Bible about people who were possessed with demons and evil spirits and how Jesus commanded them to leave.

We definitely need Jesus to intervene because I can't do anything to help Renee except pray, I thought. The truth was, I didn't want to be there to see what was happening right before my eyes. I was definitely out of my comfort zone.

Tonya leaned down to touch Renee's shoulder as she continued to pray. I began praying that God would heal Renee's body and that if any evil thing was trying to destroy her, He would free her in Jesus' name. I squatted beside her and placed my hand lightly on her back as I prayed. I closed my eyes.

I began to feel an eerie air around me. When I opened my eyes, Renee, dressed in her navy skirt and jacket, flipped onto her back without using her arms or hands. Instantly her eyes popped open.

I think my heart stopped. I was face-to-face with someone or something that could make Renee wiggle and flip like a rag doll and slither on the ground. Her pupils were a bright red—not like blood, but like fire.

Her eyes burned into mine. I blinked and prayed harder than I'd ever known I could pray.

In a moment's time, Renee blinked and everything was back to normal. She put her hands on the floor and pushed herself to a sitting position.

"What happened?" She tugged at her jacket and pulled her skirt back down to a modest length.

We helped her to her feet. I let Tonya do the talking.

"You passed out while we were praying for you. Do you remember in the Bible in the book of Luke where the demon-possessed man fell at Jesus' feet, Jesus rebuked the demon, and it left the man?"

"Yes, my friend told me that story last week." Renee brushed her hair back in place with her hands.

"Well, we had to ask Jesus to do that for you." Tonya spoke in a soft tone.

Surprisingly, Renee raised her hands and danced around, shouting, "I'm free, I'm free, I am finally free! Thank you, thank you!"

She grabbed us and hugged us.

"We are so excited for you and are glad you are feeling better, but I need to make sure you understand it wasn't Tonya or me who did this. You should be thanking Jesus," I said to Renee.

"Oh, I do, I do!"

I touched her arm. "I need to know if you have accepted Jesus as your Lord and Savior."

She calmed down. Her countenance was relaxed. "I've read my Bible and wondered whether or not to believe Jesus could heal me, but I just couldn't trust anyone with this darkness I felt inside."

I opened my Bible and read her the most simple, yet most powerful verse I could think of. "Look, John 3:16 says, 'For God so loved the world that he gave his one and only Son, that whoever believes in him shall not perish but have eternal life' (NIV). Are you ready to trust Jesus now that He has set you free?"

Renee accepted Jesus as her Savior and left the church singing. I was relieved but energized to see God deliver Renee from this demon that had possessed her.

I struggled and had nightmares about this incident for a while. Those red eyes haunted me. I prayed more than I'd prayed before, and I trusted God to deliver me from the imprint of those devilish eyes. He did just that.

Since that day I've experienced many situations, but I've never again witnessed red eyes. I've experienced growth in my prayer life and faith, and I have prayed with many people, but with the understanding that only God, through the blood of Jesus, has the power to save, heal, and set captives free. I am nothing without Him.

The Midnight Traveler

LINDA HOWTON,
AS TOLD TO JOYCE GATTON

My job in the IT department's command center for a grocery distribution center required me to work the late shift. Nothing terribly noteworthy happened at my office, except for the occasional visit of a stray dog or tiny tree frogs that strolled or hopped in uninvited through the open back door in the summertime.

I guess we had a few murders occur if you count the accidental stomping deaths of a few frogs. But the murder mysteries were easily solved by the appearance of little frog hands, which stuck out from under the edge of the murderers' shoes.

So mostly my late shift work drummed on from night to night. My workweek started on Sunday evenings. One particular November Sunday seemed no different from others.

Because of the late hours we worked, we usually had a laid-back atmosphere. I had a good camaraderie with my three male co-workers. When time came to pass the day's work to the oncoming shift, however, we were always glad to stand at the time clock and wait for the midnight hour to toll so we could head home.

Our cars were parked in front of the well-lit office, and the four of us always walked out together. On this cold November night my supervisor and I chatted as we walked to my car. We said good-night, and he walked to his car a couple of parking spaces away while I opened my car door. I was happy to be getting into my new Chevy Lumina for my fifteen-mile trip home.

The interior light came on, and I glanced into the empty backseat as I slipped behind the steering wheel. Breathing in the cold November air, I backed out of the parking space and headed for home, thinking of my warm bed.

I pulled out from the frontage drive and onto the main street that ran north and south. My four car doors had automatically locked, so I felt safe enough driving home by myself on the same route I'd been using for twenty years. I headed north over the bridge that crossed the Kansas River, then rounded the curve on the exit ramp going west onto Kansas Highway 32.

Suddenly, when I made the turn onto the exit ramp, I felt the presence of a person in the car with me. I knew that couldn't be the case. My car was clearly empty when I unlocked it in the parking lot.

However, the feeling of someone else's presence kept getting stronger and stronger. And stranger yet, I had a total absence of fear.

I continued heading west toward home, merging onto the divided highway. I saw no other cars, which was normal for the midnight ride home. The Kansas River and a set of railroad tracks ran parallel to me on my left, and a few closed businesses were on my right. A small bakery, car lot, grocery store, the post office, and a couple of bars were all dark. The tall streetlights illuminated the road and my car.

Finally, I was so overcome with the immediate presence of someone in the backseat that I turned to look. Sitting behind the passenger's seat was a young man who appeared to be in his early twenties. He smiled at me as if he were extremely happy to be in the car with me. He didn't say a word.

He had short brown hair and a perfectly trimmed brown beard. He was wearing a heavy, collared, long tweed coat, buttoned down the front. He looked immaculate. His hands seemed to rest in his lap, although I couldn't see them. I had to turn back around to watch the road in front of me; I was driving about fifty-five miles per hour. I noticed the dead grass in the median strip as I drove on. The businesses became fewer and fewer, and the homes along that stretch of the road sat back a long way from the highway.

I knew I wasn't in a dream. I was clearly aware of the scenery passing me. However, I was traveling with a man who could not possibly be mortal. My emotional state was one of elation.

There's a man in my car! There's a man in my car! There's a man in my car! I kept saying to myself.

It was as if I was singing the words to a song over and over. I turned around to look at him again. He still had that joyful smile on his face, and I felt incredible peace. In fact, I'd never felt such ultimate tranquility before. I was so overcome with the joy that appeared on his face that I didn't think about asking him who he was and why he had appeared to me. The longer I drove, the more the sense of peace, joy, and tranquility overpowered me.

A few minutes later I looked at the man again. He communicated to me, not with an audible voice but from his mind to my mind, "I'm just going to ride with you for a little while."

It was so amazing. Who would ever believe me? Surely no one in his or her right mind would. I continued to drive and turned to look at him again. The same joyful smile greeted me. The muscles in my face started to tire as I realized I had been smiling a huge smile ever since I felt his presence.

Because I was so astounded at his appearing and was filled with complete calm, the obvious need to ask why he was there simply didn't hit me. But I didn't need to ask in order to know he wasn't from Kansas.

The surrounding countryside became sparsely populated. Still several miles from home, I entered the small town of Edwardsville, with its one and only stoplight. When I stopped at the light, I suddenly knew the man was no longer in my car. The overwhelming peace of his presence left.

For fear of being thought a lunatic, I didn't even tell my husband about this for several weeks. I gradually told a few people who I didn't think would try to have me committed. One person advised me not to tell anyone, which fueled my trepidation.

Another reason I didn't tell people was that when I did relay the event, I couldn't seem to do so without sobbing—not from sadness, but from sheer emotion.

I had driven that path countless times at all different hours of the night. Never before or in the nine years after did anyone else appear. I can only speculate that God sent this man to protect me from a danger that night, from something I had no way of knowing was in my path.

I have not given up trying to understand the "why" of it. Sometimes when I am driving alone I think of it. At times when I start to doubt God's presence, He immediately draws me back to that night. Then I remember the man's face and the peace I felt. It brings me a renewed level of comfort each time I need it.

One of the duties of angels is to protect us, and I believe on that dark, lonely road one was commissioned to "ride with me for a little while" to accomplish a purpose I will never fully realize in this life.

The Mysterious Blonde

M. JEANETTE SHARP

The tall, slender blonde wiped her eyes as she hurried past the narrow window next to the office door. The upturned collar of her black overcoat shielded her face, so I had no idea who she was. The only door beyond the main office door was the private entry my sister used for her office on the ninth floor of the medical center.

I scanned the appointment book, but there was no appointment scheduled, so I had no clue who the mystery woman might be. The incident sparked my curiosity.

It must be a distraught patient who wishes her visit to a psychiatrist's office kept private, I decided.

I didn't normally work in my sister's office. However, her phone call that morning had interrupted my devotional time.

"Jeanette, Chris needs to take the day off, and I need your help. Could you fill in for her today?" she had asked.

I glanced at my schedule and said, "Sure. See you at nine."

The round clock on the kitchen wall read 7:00 a.m.— time enough to wrap up my devotionals, eat breakfast, and dash through my morning routine. Then I headed to my sister's office, where I occasionally helped with administrative work.

The medical building that housed Twilah's office perched on a hilltop overlooking the city. I pulled my car into Chris's empty parking space and entered the building.

Keys in hand, I turned the lock on the office door and stepped inside. As I glanced around the room at scattered magazines, crumpled gum wrappers, chairs in disarray, and used coffee cups, I realized the first task was to tidy the reception area. Next I made a fresh pot of coffee, selected Vivaldi's *Four Seasons* on CD, and pushed Play on the Bosch sound system.

The office door in the next room clicked, signaling my sister's arrival. Minutes later she leaned around the corner. "Hi. The coffee smells wonderful. I had a cup earlier at home, but the aroma of your fresh brew calls for another."

"One cup, just the way you like it, coming right up."

"Any messages?"

"The answering service forwarded three calls. I'll bring the messages in with your coffee."

After I placed the coffee and messages on Twilah's desk, I hugged her. She studied the call list and said, "I need to return these. When the first patient arrives, ask him to be seated for a few minutes. I'll signal when I'm ready."

A short time later, I greeted her first appointment of the day. "Good morning, Mr. Simmons. Dr. Fox will be with you shortly. May I offer you a cup of coffee?"

The morning whisked by with patients coming and going. I stayed busy. By noon my stomach grumbled its discontent. Normally Twilah and I left the office for lunch, but today something was different. The door to her office remained closed.

That's when I noticed the mysterious blonde hurry past to Twilah's office. Her surreptitious visit must have something to do with the messages left with the answering service, I decided.

As I mulled over the mystery, the office door opened and Twilah walked toward the front desk, purse in hand. "Let's run to the bistro for lunch. I'm starving."

"Sounds good to me." She said nothing about the mysterious visitor.

After lunch the afternoon whizzed by. We closed the office on Tuesdays at 3:00 so that Twilah had plenty of time to prepare for the evening Bible study she led.

I planned to arrive early that night to grab my usual front-row seat at the Bible study, but I was detained. The sounds of worship music greeted me in the parking lot. I slipped into a chair near the back of the room and joined the singing. As the music ended, I glanced around the room. That's when I saw Kathy Monroe holding a newborn baby. That surprised me because the Monroes had no children.

The Monroes were new to the Bible study, and while I had not met them, I knew they owned a chain of furniture stores, and I frequently saw their television ads. Rick's tall frame, dark hair, and olive complexion contrasted with Kathy's soft blue eyes, fair skin, and porcelain-like features. They were a striking couple.

I scanned the rest of the crowd for familiar faces and looked again at Kathy, but this time there was no baby!

I tried to make sense of it. Had my eyes played tricks on me? Could I have been mistaken? Neither she nor Rick held a baby, and no baby was anywhere around them. But I knew I had seen a baby in her arms!

My focus on the evening's lesson went out the window. I kept searching for a logical explanation of what I knew I had seen. My thoughts played and replayed the mysterious sequence of events.

Twilah's final "Amen" brought me out of my stupor. People collected their belongings and prepared to leave. Some lingered around Twilah to discuss the lesson; others chatted with friends as they moved toward the door at a snail's pace.

I tried to reach Twilah, slowed by the flow of people coming toward me as they left the room. But my strange experience needed answers, and when I reached Twilah I said, "Something I can't explain happened tonight. I saw Kathy Monroe holding a newborn baby."

"Go tell her; she needs to hear this!" Twilah insisted.

I saw the Monroes inching their way down the aisle. Armed with Twilah's encouragement, I approached them. I extended my hand to Kathy and said, "Hi, I don't believe we've met. I'm Jeanette Sharp, Dr. Fox's sister."

Their warm response eased my awkwardness. "Kathy, during tonight's meeting, I had a strange experience. I saw you holding a newborn baby."

Kathy's hand flew to cover her mouth and tears filled her eyes. She looked from me to Rick. The glow on their faces spoke volumes.

Twilah approached us, smiling. "Did you tell them?"

"Yes."

"Kathy, I would like to share the full story with Jeanette."

Kathy nodded her approval.

"This morning Kathy came to see me just before lunch," Twilah explained. "She's had several previous miscarriages and is pregnant now. Yesterday she began to show symptoms of losing this baby, too, so today I prayed with her for a full-term delivery of a healthy baby."

"So you're the mysterious blonde I saw this morning!"

Filled with a new peace in their hearts, the Monroes left that evening with the confident assurance their prayers had been answered.

During my drive home, I pondered the mystery of all that had happened with an expanded sense of awe at God's greatness.

Eight months later, Kathy gave birth to a healthy baby, just as the Lord had shown me, and I remembered Joel 2:28–29: "I will pour out my Spirit upon all people. Your sons and daughters will prophesy. Your old men will dream dreams, and your young men will see visions. In those days I will pour out my Spirit even on servants—men and women alike."

I was thrilled to realize that the Holy Spirit still gives visions to reassure people in their times of need, and I was thrilled and humbled that He had chosen to use me.

The Impotent Imp

Jan Dixon Sykes

My eyes were closed tightly when the three-foot imp arced through my open bedroom door to the side of my bed, where I lay sleeping. He stopped near my pillow and perched a foot off the floor to glare over me with unadulterated hatred.

Barely twenty, I had experienced only love and safety until this point. I was like an innocent fawn that was more curious about a hunter than aware of the danger.

So a horrific demon appearing so close to me in my subconscious mind didn't even wake me from my dream. In it, I could see both the imp peering over me with its murderous intent, and my own body resting on my side in an easy sleep.

Very soon the evil spirit's hunger to slay me jelled into a plan to choke me to death. He stuck out his claw-like finger and drew a line across my neck with the side of his spiked nail. The sensation of the touch jolted me awake.

Completely alert and heart racing, I instantly twisted toward the apparition glowering at me. He was as real while I was awake as he had been while I slept. I didn't bother examining his transparent features to figure out if he exactly matched the pictures of imps I had seen. The seething flame in his eyes held me captive.

Like the fawn that sometimes stupidly freezes the first time it realizes it is in danger, I stupidly froze.

The imp communicated with me telepathically. He was not a dream and he wanted to kill me. He hated me simply because I was a Christian. I was a threat to his kingdom. He had not been forced to visit me; he embraced his task with sadistic gusto.

As his full agenda sank in, a foreign thought sprouted into my mind: *He can't hurt you. You are covered by the blood.*

That notion immediately soothed me and gave me courage. Although my heart still pumped rapidly, I now met the demon's gaze with confidence.

One could say he blinked first—except he didn't have eyelids.

What he did, though, was begin a backward arc through the door from which he had entered. He didn't turn to leave. He faced me, eyes defiant, during his entire journey out the top of my door and into the night.

The whole episode ended quickly. However, because of the adrenaline surge it caused, twenty minutes passed before the blood pulsating in my head subsided.

How odd that my heart is still racing even though the thought about the blood calmed me. So what was the deal about the blood? Am I coated in it? I wonder if the imp could see it.

No answers came, but peaceful sleep did.

That incident happened almost forty years ago. I still have no idea why the supernatural window opened for me in that moment. I could speculate that the experience made me fearless. Except, reared inside God's insulated cocoon, I had already felt invincible before the imp's appearance.

What intrigued me more than the demon was the imprint in my mind about the blood. I had grown up singing, "There is power, power, wonder-working power, in the blood, of the Lamb." I also knew Revelation 7:14, which states, "These are they who have come out of the great tribulation; they have washed their robes and made them white in the blood of the Lamb" (NIV).

But I sure hadn't assimilated blood idioms into my schoolgirl vernacular.

Besides, any focus on salvation by blood seemed a bit macabre. Was Christ's blood a detergent? Was I dripping with blood? Did the demon see this blood and stop at my skin, the way the death angel had stopped at the bloody Passover doorposts?

Then ten years ago I found a book by a surgeon, Dr. Paul Brand, explaining why the Bible belabored the point about blood. According to Dr. Brand, our circulatory system is an analogy of how God's plan of forgiveness and justification works. Human blood has no natural immunities and dies if exposed to disease. We would need repeated blood transfusions to replenish us with pure blood.

Christ came to this world not just to offer His pure blood, but also to take all our diseases upon himself and to build up antibodies within His blood. That way, when we take in His blood—even symbolically—we, too, are immunized and liberated to move about without worrying that some offense might befall us. As His perfect blood floods into our veins, it attacks and kills each germ (sin). With each heartbeat, His blood washes away all iniquities.

Bitterness, envy, greed, pride, lust, gluttony, and more—His blood has overcome these worldly epidemics. That explains why the demon hadn't been able to kill me. He couldn't penetrate his contamination into my system. The divine blood in me more than conquered him. All the imp could touch was the outside of my skin. I wasn't even wounded from his trespass.

Even to this day my spirit is not wounded. Of course, I've been through all the modern-day trials—broken relationships, cancer, job loss, relocation. My skin shows the scars. But through all the hardships, I have remained emotionally intact. Christ's blood has kept me, maybe not free from pain, but free from being completely shattered by anything. And it still makes me feel invincible.

The Angel on the Wall

Carolyn D. Poindexter

My marriage was shot. We had everything against us: in-law conflict, financial challenges, babies early in the marriage. The circumstances overwhelmed our dreams and expectations very shortly after the honeymoon phase.

We were very young and had been married for only three years. We had two little girls in tow, and the pressures of a young family on one meager income were quite challenging. We had thought we could sail through anything undaunted, with love getting us through. But that was when we were dating and dreaming about how it would be once we married.

As reality hit, disagreements occurred more frequently—until we finally decided to separate. Exasperated, I moved back in with my parents while I debated whether to continue with my marriage.

We tried hard to patch it up, but then Michael was laid off his job. Keeping up with the rent and bills became impossible and caused more disagreements. We had discussions about reuniting, but we couldn't come to a meeting of the minds about the issues that thwarted our efforts.

Love wasn't one of the issues. There was no doubt that we both loved each other very much and wanted to make our marriage work. But Michael's job loss made the dream of reuniting seem even more of a fantasy. We were young and easily influenced by external ideals. It seemed as though our prayers about our situation were going unheard.

Trying to mend what seemed irretrievably broken, we began attending a weekly Bible study together at a friend's home every Friday. We enjoyed the strength we gleaned from the seasoned members of the group.

One night we had a new visitor—a pastor my husband knew from high school but hadn't seen since then. That evening, before the study, they chatted about old school memories and "whatever happened to . . ."

When Alex asked what my husband was currently doing, he explained that he and I were separated—and that he had been laid off his job and was trying to find another one so that we could get our lives back together.

"Aw, man, I'm sorry to hear that. You look like such a happy couple. I never would have guessed you were going through so much. But it's good you're keeping God in your lives. And as long as you love each other, you can make it through this," Alex said.

"Yes," I chimed in, "but it seems like the harder we pray, the worse it becomes."

Michael agreed as he held my hand.

"Have you ever tried fasting?" Alex asked.

"No, what's that about?" Michael responded.

The conversation led to our Bible study being about fasting and prayer that night. I had fasted before and was well acquainted with the sacrifice bringing positive results.

My husband decided to fast beginning that night, and I didn't tell him, but I decided to fast with him. I wanted my marriage back, and this was sort of a last-ditch effort to mend it. Nothing else had seemed to work, and I wanted to know how to do it to get the very best results. I also wanted to know if I was on the right track with my prayers.

I needed to be sure, now more than ever, that we could make it, and if so, how should we proceed? It took faith to believe that fasting would help. I faced the decision to continue with my marriage and try to make it work no matter what, or to try to make it alone with my two little girls, who were only one and two. I felt it was a tough decision either way.

Later that night I tucked the kids in, then climbed into my bed and prayed until I fell asleep. A short while later, I opened my eyes for seemingly no reason. Typically when I awoke from a deep sleep, it would take a minute or so to drift into awareness. But this night my eyes popped open, and I was fully conscious. I stared at the window as the street lamp dimly shined through the curtain. Then I lifted my head and looked straight up.

There, on the wall, was an angel.

He was in a seated position, staring at me. I couldn't see what he was sitting on, but he seemed comfortable and securely positioned.

I don't really know why I refer to the angel as "he." He didn't appear to be either male or female. Nevertheless, he was dressed in a long, white robe and sported a wavy, golden, shoulder-length bob. His clothes, hair, and skin emitted a soft, bright glow that lit up the entire space where he sat, only inches from me.

"Michael will find a job. Keep fasting. Keep praying," he said matter-of-factly.

And just as suddenly as he appeared, the light was gone and so was the angel. The only sound in the room was the beat of my heart, which seemed about to jump out of my chest.

I couldn't believe what I had just seen. It was very real and I was immediately terribly afraid. I wanted to run to my parents' room, climb into their bed, and bury my face in a pillow, but I was stunned, too afraid to move. Surprisingly, I fell fast asleep only moments later.

Around 6:00 a.m. Michael called me, so excited he could barely speak! A contractor had just asked him to report to work immediately and offered a salary far better than he had previously made. It was Saturday morning. Who makes business calls and hires on a Saturday?

He sounded so hopeful. He wanted me to know that God had already answered our prayers. I was in shock at the sudden news—proof that what the angel had said had surely come to pass.

I told him that I had fasted with him and that an angel had visited only hours before. We were silent for a few moments.

It had all happened so fast. We agreed to talk about it, and the new job, later that evening.

I thank God for His mindfulness of the things that matter to me. When we diligently sought Him, He quickly answered. He sent me verification that I was indeed going in the right direction with my prayers and fasting in a way that I could not doubt. He knew what it would take for me to trust in Him to go further in the direction He was sending us, without any more reservation.

Our challenges and fasting showed Michael that God really did exist—and that He loved us and indeed answered our prayers. The Bible, through prayer and fasting, became real to him.

I never saw that angel again, but I continue to have times of fasting to this day, forty years later. And it wasn't the last time that I saw God's handiwork in my life. Indeed, it was only the beginning. Yet each time I'm amazed at how He works things out, step by step, in His way, when we trust Him.

Divine GPS

DALE L. DRAGOMIR

"Call him." The urge was unmistakable and compelling. If I obeyed, would it lead to a miracle or embarrassment? Nothing within sight was moving, and all I heard was the buzzing of insects on a hot Carolina August day. What did I have to lose? Cranking up my courage, I called, "Samson!"

This odd journey had begun months earlier. Samson was an energetic yellow Labrador less than a year old. The awkward puppy stage for big dogs sometimes lasts longer than pet owners anticipate, and Samson was a handful.

Living up to his biblical namesake, he was muscular and powerful. He was also headstrong. He wouldn't walk on a leash and seldom came when called. Because of his wild ways and our two cats, he was banished from the house—except at night when compassion overcame our fears of his wreaking havoc.

Samson had become a member of our household somewhat against our will. He had been adopted by a young woman from the church I pastored. Terri had a sparkling personality and was full of life, but she often questioned whether God truly loved her. When she fell on hard times we invited her to live with us until she could get back on her feet.

Samson was a part of the package, and soon he won our hearts with his loving, lively temperament. I often smiled in anticipation of his exuberant greeting when I arrived home, and I secretly wished he would not soon be moving out.

When our family went on summer vacation, we left Terri in charge of the house, the dog, and our two cats. We knew she would enjoy the privacy and independence. On the trip home, I was looking forward to one of my vigorous romps with Samson. But when we pulled into the driveway, we saw only his yard stake and a long, empty chain.

I called Terri at work, and she began sobbing. She had taken Samson for a visit to her family and turned him loose in the fenced backyard. She didn't realize the back gate had been left open, and the dog bolted. He was gone in a yellow flash, and though Terri called repeatedly, he did not come. She had already searched for days, driving the neighborhood streets and calling his name. Repeated trips to the dog pound were fruitless. Samson was gone.

For most dog lovers, pets are companions and friends. For Terri, Samson was much more than that. He brought her a special joy during difficult days, and she had often wept out her problems at night while clinging to his soft fur. He had become a symbol of God's blessing. Caring for him brought a comforting rhythm to her life, and his silly antics made her hard times much more bearable.

"I don't understand why God would take him from me now," she cried. "Everything is finally looking better, and now this?"

She was devastated and asked if she was being punished for the sins of her past, even though she had been forgiven.

I mumbled affirmations of God's love, but I shared her loss too much to understand God's purposes at the moment. Everything I said seemed canned and trite. I prayed with her briefly that the dog would be found and tried to focus on the sermon I would preach on Sunday.

Terri changed. Usually she was bubbly and cheerful at church, her laughter bouncing off the sanctuary walls. That week she was stone-faced. Resentment flashed from her eyes, and no protestations that she was fine were believable.

When pressed, Terri released her thoughts in fiery phrases, betraying her true emotions.

"Obviously, God doesn't love me as much as I thought He did," she said. "If He cares so much about every little thing I feel, then He wouldn't let me lose the one thing in my life that meant something to me."

Her heart was hardening by the minute. We had to find that dog.

My wife and I prayed fervently. Night and day our pleadings ascended to heaven.

"Let Samson find his way home."

"Help Terri spot him somewhere."

Finally, we prayed, "Let *us* find him."

We drove to her parents' neighborhood, scoured the streets, and called, to no avail. We knew we were asking the impossible. Samson was wearing a collar, but he had no tags that would identify his owner. He was such a friendly, appealing animal. Someone had probably found him, and he was enjoying a wonderful new life. After a few days our faith flagged. It seemed like time to give up.

Everywhere I drove, I looked for Samson. Sometimes it seemed yellow Labs were everywhere, but none was the dog I sought.

One day a couple of weeks after Samson disappeared, I had to travel an interstate highway to visit a parishioner in the hospital. Even though I knew it was too far for Samson to have traveled, I scanned the fields on my way home as best I could at a high rate of speed. There was no sign of him. My words to God had long since run out. I prayed only by the yearning in my heart.

Suddenly, my foot hit the brake, almost unbidden. I had a powerful urge to exit the highway, and I yielded. Sitting at the end of the ramp, I heard an inner voice: *Turn right.*

I turned the wheel, while telling myself this was foolish. Soon I saw an intersection. *Turn left.* My wild experiment continued with several more turns, and I began to wonder if my prayers had given birth to an obsession. Eventually I heard, *Stop here.*

I turned off the engine and heard only silence. Getting out of the car, I scanned the horizon, even though my brain told me I was losing my sanity. Then came the compelling command: *Call him.*

I'm well known for my preacher's voice, powerful and clear. I didn't use it at first. Timidly, I called, "Samson!"

It felt right. I walked a few steps closer to the empty field in front of me and called louder, "Samson!"

A wild, leafy commotion broke the summer stillness, and an enormous yellow dog exploded from the bushes. He nearly knocked me down with his excitement. I hugged and wrestled him, and there was no mistake. It was Terri's dog!

Dumbfounded, I received an explanation from the man who ran out of the thicket after Samson. Smiling and shaking my hand, the truck driver told me how he had seen the dog trotting down the highway. Fearing the dog would be struck and killed, he pulled over to investigate. Soon the thirsty but content dog was riding beside him in the front seat, and they continued to his country home about twenty miles away.

The trucker had posted ads trying to find Samson's owner—it was obvious the dog had been well cared for, and he knew someone would have been heartbroken over losing him. But no answer had been received.

"There you go, boy. I knew someone would come for you," growled the trucker. He looked strangely at me, then asked, "How did you find him?"

I swallowed hard and explained as best I could. It sounded farfetched even to me.

"Well, God moves in mysterious ways," the man said, and I couldn't agree fast enough.

Samson panted, shed, and slobbered in my front seat, and I didn't care. I was speeding as I returned to my hometown with the giant, goofy dog unaware that he was the centerpiece of a miracle. Wanting their reunion to be a memorable one, I pulled up at home and left Samson in the car. Grinning, I rang the doorbell.

Terri opened the door, her features expressionless.

"There's someone in the car who wants to see you," I said.

Terri glanced toward the driveway, her eyes flew open wide, and her hand shot up to cover her mouth. I don't know what words wanted to come out, but evidently she didn't want the preacher to hear them.

I seized the moment of her surprise to sprint to the car and open the door before Samson tore it off. Terri fell to her knees and the dog covered her with licks and slurps, perhaps enjoying the taste of her salty tears.

I've relived the joy of those spectacular minutes several times in the years since then. Soon after they were reunited, Terri and Samson moved out. Apartment life didn't suit the energetic dog, and Terri found Samson a loving home where he could romp unencumbered.

Terri did not lose her faith. She married, had children, and started her own childcare business. She still refers to the Samson years as "dark days," but I know that God sent one bright, yellow-tinged ray of light to pierce that darkness at just the right moment. He demonstrated to Terri just how much He delights in lavishing His love upon His children, especially the ones who think they don't deserve it.

Whenever I get a strong urge that doesn't seem to make sense, I remember that a big, wild dog taught me to listen carefully. It just might be the voice of God.

Shelter From the Storm

DEB WUETHRICH

We were enjoying a summer weekend at one of New York's Finger Lakes when my husband sat on the edge of the bed.

"I don't feel right," he said. It was unusual for him to admit such a thing, and even more so for him to willingly get into the car to head for a nearby community hospital.

Doctors found he had an erratic heartbeat and arranged to transfer him to Strong Memorial Hospital in Rochester for more tests. I followed the ambulance for the forty-five-minute trip, praying all the while to a God I'd not been very close to in recent years, though I grew up attending Sunday school.

At Strong, doctors determined Gordy had a blockage that would require a stent. The surgery went well, but in his room, Gordy grew agitated and tried to rip out tubes and

IV lines. He was compromising the point at his wrist where they'd entered an artery. He acted strangely and complained of a terrible headache. Sometimes I couldn't understand his garbled words.

His increasing agitation roiled like the gray clouds before a storm at the lake.

"Shhh. Calm down. It will be okay," I told him as he kept grabbing his aching head.

The storm continued to rage as doctors came in and asked my husband if he knew today's date.

"Of course I do!" he snapped with obvious disdain, and gave a date from the 1960s.

"How do you make your living?" they asked.

His words came out garbled while he looked at the medical team as if they were deaf or dumb for not understanding him. He tried to let them know he had a PhD and was not as stupid as they seemed to think he was.

As Gordy's irritation grew, a neurologist pulled me aside.

"We think he's had a stroke," he said. "It's one of the risks with the procedure your husband had."

The rest of the team looked at me with pity, while some avoided eye contact.

"You'll have to accept that your life has just changed forever," one young fellow stated. "He'll need a lot of help and will have to go into a rehabilitation center."

I was stunned.

How can this be happening? He was fine just a little while ago.

Late that night an orderly wheeled Gordy to the hospital's basement to attempt an MRI. I sat in the silent bowels of the facility, hearing only my husband's groans, cries, and even screams.

"Make it stop!" my husband cried as he held his head and tried to turn away from the glaring overhead lights in the hall.

My world was crumbling, but I sensed a nudge to pray—and to pray as I hadn't in years. I remember asking God's forgiveness first for the distance I'd allowed to grow between us. We talked about how I had drifted from faith—a faith once strong enough to believe in miracles.

"That's what Gordy needs now, Lord," I prayed. "He needs a miracle."

That's what I'll do. I'll believe for one right now, I thought, and hoped God would know that I really wanted to come closer to Him again. I realized it was the sort of eleventh-hour bargaining people make in desperate moments, but I kept praying—there in the basement and later as I drifted to sleep in Gordy's room after they'd given him medication to quiet him.

I awoke to a rustling. Gordy was awake and staring at me, puzzled. He recited the date and then repeated it.

"Right?" he asked, hesitantly.

"Yes," I confirmed, elated.

"They asked me yesterday," he said. "I gave the wrong answer, didn't I?"

I was amazed that he remembered this. I noticed then that he was also speaking clearly. He wanted help to the bathroom—and he was hungry.

My heart leaped with joy! God had heard my prayers, and He'd answered dramatically. He'd given us the miracle! Still, I hoped it wasn't just a temporary reprieve.

Soon, the neurologist's assistant came in on morning rounds. She had a confused look on her face as she examined Gordy and asked him questions. She disappeared and the neurologist breezed in.

"I couldn't believe it, so I had to see this for myself!" he exclaimed. "We were sure it was a stroke. But it looks like he's going to be fine."

The interns and physicians made their rounds, each amazed at Gordy's turnaround. A couple of them looked skeptical as I said, "God answered my prayer for a miracle." One tried to explain, "Sometimes things happen and we can't really say why." But I knew it was God's doing.

Within two days, we were on our way back home to Michigan. Gordy had medication and instructions regarding his heart condition, but by God's grace we were not headed to rehab as the result of a stroke. I got my husband back for several more years after I prayed for a miracle in that basement.

Through this experience, God not only showed us where to seek shelter from the storm—in Him—but also, through the extraordinary outcome, showed us how to seek peace. His safe haven became a regular destination for me and later for Gordy, too—a place where a gentle wind can soothe a lost and hurting heart and provide generously for our needs, even when we think all hope is gone.

A Two-Captive Release

P. R. JARAMILLO

Dad ruled the household with an iron fist, driven by fear and arrogance and fueled by occasional bouts with alcohol. He swept obstacles aside as if they were trivial annoyances—not seeming to care that those obstacles were often his wife and children.

His presence elicited a variety of emotions in me: fear, hurt, anxiety, and once in a while something I couldn't quite identify. When I grew older I realized it was sadness and compassion. Those feelings persisted long after my parents divorced and I married and moved out of state.

During one of my yearly trips to see Mom, I impulsively decided to drive the additional hour to visit Dad. This was something I had never done before. As an adult, my contact with him was limited to occasional meetings at my siblings' homes.

I expected to spend an uncomfortable hour trying to keep the conversation on neutral ground. But I was completely unprepared for the disturbing and far-reaching impact the visit would have on both of us.

After greeting him, I sat on the chair nearest the door. He sat on the sofa opposite me and talked about people we both knew. My replies were brief and careful. I wanted to keep the conversation on a light note. But no matter how I responded or what topic I introduced, he found fault and ridiculed anyone or anything that crossed his mind, whether they were part of the initial conversation or not.

Half an hour into the visit I made an excuse to leave. I was crossing the street when I realized I had left my keys and purse next to the chair where I was sitting. I retraced my steps and was about to call out to him through the open door. Instead I stopped abruptly and gasped!

He was lying on the sofa, curled up in a fetal position. His back was toward me. He must have heard my gasp because he turned and struggled to sit up. I mumbled something about my purse as I stepped through the doorway.

I picked it up and started to leave, then stopped and looked back at him. His look of defiance was firmly in place and seemed more pronounced than usual. I struggled to find something appropriate to say. Finally I said the first words that came to my mind: "Can I pray with you before I leave?"

He ignored my question. I sat next to him and mumbled a brief prayer, barely aware of what I was saying. Tears were streaming down my face when my prayer ended. In a spontaneous gesture, I reached up and laid my palm against his cheek. His eyes softened and with unexpected tenderness he said, "Don't cry, my daughter."

I drove away struggling to reconcile my childhood perception of Dad as an all-powerful giant with my glimpse of him lying helpless in a fetal position. I longed to help him but at the same time knew he would belittle any effort I made on his behalf.

Even the suggestion that he needed help would be repugnant to him. He had spent his entire life living behind a facade of pride and belligerence. He was not about to let it go.

I drove to Mom's house. She probably noticed my tumultuous emotions, but neither of us said anything. Any mention of Dad always caused her to become defensive. I longed for the peace and safety of my own home.

I returned home expecting to put the incident behind me, but a heavy weight seemed to permanently lodge in my heart. I thought about Dad constantly. I prayed for him several times a day, but instead of lifting, the burden intensified. I sent him cards and small gifts and, on one occasion, a Bible with key passages highlighted. He didn't respond.

My concern for him moved beyond worrying about his physical and emotional health, or even the shock of seeing him looking vulnerable, to a feeling of doom. Sometimes I felt that God was preparing me for something, at other times I felt like I was whirling toward a dark abyss.

Forces stronger than I had ever encountered were pulling me in opposite directions. I was not sleeping well and my weight dropped considerably.

One morning after I returned from driving my children to school, I shut the front door and fell to my knees. I cried loudly, asking the Lord to lift the burden I had carried for months. I prayed for Dad again and again and asked God to use me on his behalf. I continued praying until I felt a deep sense of assurance and the heaviness lifted.

A year later my brother called to say that Dad was at his house for a couple of days. When our conversation ended, I set the receiver down with a deep sigh. The emotions I thought had been resolved began to reappear with an added twist. I had never invited Dad to our home because I feared his presence would bring disaster. Now I began to wonder if God was asking me to do the very thing I dreaded.

Surely not, I told myself. *God understands my need for security.*

In bed that night I tossed and turned. My prayers alternated between a resigned, "Thy will be done, Lord," and a rebellious, "No! You cannot ask this of me." I had vivid nightmares in which I relived violent scenes from my childhood.

Throughout the night, the cycle of resignation, nightmare, and rebellion replayed itself again and again. Morning finally dawned and with it my decision.

Sharing the message of salvation with Dad is the important thing, I told myself.

On the way to my brother's house that evening, the Lord began to nudge me again, this time with a Bible verse from Isaiah 61:1: "He has sent me to comfort the brokenhearted and to proclaim that captives will be released." And another from Matthew 25:35: "I was a stranger, and you invited me into your home."

"Okay." I spoke the word more out of frustration than conviction. "I'll invite him, but if he makes even one disparaging remark, I'll withdraw my invitation immediately."

When I arrived at my brother's house, I noticed a change in Dad's attitude. He was quieter than usual. His belligerent demeanor was not as evident. When I invited him to our house, he smiled and accepted readily.

At home I baked cookies and made hot chocolate while he entertained the children with stories about his childhood, which had been spent on a cattle ranch. After a couple hours of storytelling and snacking, I sent the children to bed. I pushed the empty plates and cups aside, sat on the chair opposite him, and asked, "Dad, have you accepted Christ as your Savior?"

Taken aback by my blunt question, he hesitated. Then he responded with a snicker, "Why would I want to do that?"

"Because that's the only way any of us can enter heaven."

"Is that even possible?"

"Yes," I said. "It is possible."

I was amazed that we were having this conversation, and despite his skepticism, I sensed something powerful was happening.

"So, tell me," he smirked, "what kind of penance does an old sinner like me have to do to get to heaven?"

"No penance. You just need to invite Christ into your heart."

"I suppose I have to kneel at an altar, bow down, and beg for mercy?" He laughed.

I sensed an evil force egging him to mock and rebuff what I was sharing with him. I felt the same sense of doom I had experienced when I had begun praying for him. I asked God silently for strength and protection.

"No," I said. "You can invite Christ into your life right here, right now."

His eyes bore into mine with the same piercing look that had caused me to tremble and hide as a child. I stared back. Finally, after what seemed like an eternity, he looked at his clenched hands resting on the table. The atmosphere in the room changed. The evil presence and the sense of doom receded. With a deep sigh he shook his head and said, "I've struggled all my life for a place on earth. How can a place in heaven be so easy?"

I took my Bible from the shelf behind me and read several verses I'd highlighted in the version I sent him. He countered each one with questions—some were voiced curiously, while others were laced with doubt and cynicism. Little by little, we began to establish a connection that rose above the layers of distrust and resentment that had built up between us over the years.

Just before midnight, Dad invited Christ into his heart, and somewhere in the midst of our long conversation, I released the hurt, fear, and anger that I had felt toward him for most of my life.

Peace and joy flooded my heart.

After breakfast the following day, I drove him to my brother's house. We hugged each other for the first time since I was a little child.

A few months after his visit, I boarded an airplane to my home state. Dad had suffered a massive heart attack while driving. He crashed the car into a concrete divider and died instantly.

On my way to his funeral I marveled at the grace of God and the infinite mercy with which He moves mountains to "set the captives free."

My own freedom was just as real as Dad's.

The Moveable Moose

MARGARET ANN STIMATZ

Y ou never know what the day will bring," Helen chimed, tossing gear into the Suburban.

"Well, I know what I'm doing. I'm taking in some jazz downtown later on," Mary's husband, David, announced. "You girls drive safely and have fun!"

With that, we three friends headed into an adventure we'd never forget. Mary, our avid hiker friend, had persuaded Helen and me—both inclined to enjoy the outdoors from folding chairs pitched by a stream—to join her on this day hike in Montana's Glacier National Park.

"It's an easy walk," she promised. "And absolutely gorgeous."

The drive was breathtaking, with the blue jewel of Lake McDonald, the drizzle of snowmelt cascading down the

Weeping Wall, and dazzling switchbacks along the Going-to-the-Sun Road. Our spirits soared with each mile, as if to match the rising elevation.

At the summit of Logan Pass, which was surrounded in every direction by panoramic views, we stretched our limbs and picnicked on a rock with a party of chipmunks. I snoozed in the sun while my friends browsed the gift shop. Then we started up the boardwalk trail.

What a day! Firs growing grizzled and sparse, marmots basking, golden-mantled ground squirrels scurrying, and chipmunks pirouetting on hind legs, hoping for handouts. Four clusters of bighorn sheep and a sprinkling of mountain goats posed for close-ups. Wildflower blankets stretched as far as the eye could see—whites, reds, blues, and yellows—gentian, bear grass, wild geranium, and Indian paintbrush.

Finally, saturated with joy and beauty, we piled back into the Suburban van. Through my backseat window, I saw the blend of blue skies and green thicket. Meadows and marshlands blurred as the miles rolled past.

"What would you think of stopping for dinner at—" Mary's words broke off.

My backseat reverie snapped. I saw what had interrupted Mary's thoughts.

A mother moose with a calf suddenly appeared on the road. Directly in the path of our fast-moving van.

Mary didn't have a second to blast the horn, hit the brakes, or even swerve. None of us had a moment to pray or exclaim. It happened that fast.

Suddenly I saw what seemed like a mirage: mama moose and baby, standing. Alive. Munching nonchalantly—as though nothing the least extraordinary had just occurred. And more amazingly, there they were on the *far* side, *across* the highway.

How had that happened? Mystical transposition of matter, time, or space?

What actually did transpire we'll never know this side of heaven. Time seemed to stop; laws of physics were apparently suspended. Otherwise, how could we have averted a slamming impact, shattering dismemberment, bleeding, traumatic brain injuries, or even multiple deaths?

We three gaped at the grazing pair—disbelieving, shocked, shaken. How was it possible that our world was now not only intact, but even serene? Surely some mighty unseen hand had intervened, plucking two moose and three humans from harm.

An hour later, over dinner, we revisited the experience with bewilderment, wonder, and a torrent of gratitude.

"It was like the Lord picked up those moose and plopped them down on the far side of the highway."

"At their speed and ours, there's no earthly, physical explanation why we didn't crash head on."

"What does a mama moose weigh, anyway? Wouldn't she be around eight hundred pounds? Imagine the force of impact. . . ."

We had no answers, only mysteries to ponder.

"You never know what the day will bring." As we headed back to Kalispell, my mind replayed those words, along with a visual reel of the day's glories. But my joy and gratitude began to erode, preempted by troubling questions. *Why, God? Why did you save us today? Why us? Why not that young Christian couple on motorcycles last month, parents who left two young sons tragically orphaned?*

I thought of other tragedies not averted, other lives not saved. Mercifully, my dark musings were obliterated by our arrival at Mary's, where—over slices of huckleberry pie—we poured out our amazing tale to the properly incredulous David.

Some years later, I now look back on that day and ponder lessons learned. Life is fragile, so unpredictable. In the twinkling of an eye it can be radically altered, shattered, destroyed. Our time on earth is brief, meant only to prepare us for life everlasting.

God is all-loving, all-powerful, and always sees the big picture. When His hand brings good—as in our close call with the moose—how easy it is to rejoice and give Him thanks. But what about those other times, when He allows misery, suffering, and horrible evils to occur? Then it is easy to ruminate on what is bleak, to become hopeless. To ask, as I did that night, *Why, God, do you sometimes allow horrible things to happen, especially to good people?*

To this day, God has not given me the answer I demanded. In time, however, He did give me a personal reply of a different kind. That reply has emerged—over the course of many years—as a simple two-word invitation: "Trust me."

And here lies my greatest lesson, my keenest challenge: to trust God no matter what. To trust Him whether times are bitter or sweet. When I cannot detect or understand His reasons or His ways, the bottom line remains: Will I trust Him?

When my eyes are dimmed by tears and I'm blind to the bigger picture, will I trust that He loves me, He is with me, and He is ever and always about the business of making all things new?

Ex-Marlboro Man

JAMES STUART BELL

My dad, James Stuart Bell Sr., was one of the "Greatest Generation" who went into World War II to save the world for democracy. (Although he mostly remembers playing volleyball with the girls on the beach in Southern California, where he was stationed.) During the '60s he began to climb the executive ladder at AT&T (the telephone company); today he would remind you of one of the characters from the television series *Mad Men*.

As the community-relations guy with a million-dollar personality and good looks to match, he was the face of the company, concerned about its image. He played golf with civic and community leaders, wrote speeches, and was involved in the company's stance on the issues of the day, including civil rights.

Like the advertising guys in *Mad Men*, my dad dealt with corporate image in the '60s and faced a lot of stress. One way to cope was to smoke cigarettes. (In fact, in the show, the executives try to put a positive spin on cigarette smoking when their advertising dollars are at risk.) My daughter has a picture of her grandpa from the '70s in his office with the long sideburns and jet-black, brushed-back hair—and he's clearly making a point as he flourishes a cigarette with a trail of smoke.

On the surface it may appear as the perfect image of a romantic era of progress and success. But today we realize the foolishness and naïveté on the part of smokers, as well as the devastating effects of the deadly killer nicotine. My dad, of course, didn't realize that when he first tried smoking for fun as a nine-year-old in the '30s behind Father Clancy's barn when skipping Sunday Mass, or with his navy buddies. But as the decades wore on, the demon nicotine took its toll.

My dad, of course, didn't want me to smoke, but one of the first words I learned was my toddler pronunciation of the word *cigarette*.

When I asked for a puff when I was five, he said yes just so I would be cured forever. Off I went to the toilet, gagging the whole way. (After that, my mind just couldn't fathom his attraction to those awful things!)

I could locate my dad when I lost him in a department store by the sound of his faint cough. He was a two-plus-pack-a-day Marlboro Man, although he never donned a cowboy hat and rode a horse across the wintry fields like they did on the TV ads and billboards. The noxious odor pervaded our house, and he took it with him on his clothes, along with his

Old Spice shaving lotion, when he got on and off the train from New York.

As the '60s turned into the '70s, he became passionate about quitting. He would talk about it incessantly, crumple up cigarette packs, and read about the health benefits of not smoking.

My dad came from the generation that defeated Germany and Japan and believed you could do anything you set your mind to with enough positive thinking and hard work. He'd quit for a day or a week, and once for nearly two years, but he finally realized that he depended on nicotine to help him cope with the pressures of corporate leadership. Yet he also knew that smoking was cutting years off his life.

In the summer of 1974 I had a life-transforming experience with Jesus Christ, being set free of my own drug use from the hippie era. My dad told me, "I can see the difference in your eyes; I want what you have."

He'd always been a moral, churchgoing man and prided himself on his life of integrity. But in this one area he wasn't self-sufficient or successful. He knew he'd never quit smoking cigarettes on his own. So he made a deal with me: If Jesus could heal him of smoking, he would know that what my friends and I had was for real and he would cast in his lot with us.

As a young, on-fire Jesus person with my overalls and long hair, I told him, "No problem, Dad. You just gotta believe, man. Jesus is the Great Healer."

He asked me to pray for him that evening, and after finishing I told him it was a done deal in Jesus' name. He looked at me tentatively, wanting to agree but relying primarily on my faith. He had certainly seen God's power change my life.

The next morning was a Saturday, and Dad went downstairs to fix his mid-morning breakfast of bacon, eggs, toast, orange juice, and coffee. He was a bit absent-minded, trying to plan his leisurely weekend.

My dad's first cigarette on Saturday, the one he enjoyed the most, was at the end of breakfast, as he sipped his second cup of coffee. As a matter of habit he found the Marlboros, pulled one out, and sat back to enjoy the combined caffeine and nicotine high of the weekend's true beginning.

But he couldn't even get the smoke down his throat. He snorted and sputtered and felt nauseated—kind of like youngsters who are pressured to take that first drag while their peers laugh at their body's intolerance.

This didn't make sense; was he sick? He tried again only to retch even more.

Then the light went on: *Jimmy prayed for me to be healed last night!*

Only Jesus could take the craving away and return him to his childlike state before he first puffed behind Father Clancy's barn. He got down on his knees and received Jesus as Healer, Lord, and Savior. He now knew what it meant to be set free from a bondage you are helpless to overcome.

We all have our own bondages that the Holy Spirit reveals when we put our faith in the one who broke the power of sin and death on the cross. God is patient with our weaknesses and waits on us to cease striving and come to Him.

My dad never touched a cigarette again for the next thirty-five years, living to his eighty-fifth birthday. When Jesus healed him, He healed him instantly—and now he's healed completely, at home with the Lord.

A Call Homeward

CHRISTINE HENDERSON

R ead me the story of Joan of Arc," I said to my sister. Once again she pulled the worn book on the lives of the saints from her bookcase. Sitting next to her on the bed, I listened attentively. This was far from the first time I had heard the story. I already knew it by heart. Almost daily I would ask my sister to read me stories from that book. The accounts of those devout people who loved God amazed me. I was in awe of how they prayed daily and often heard His voice. How I wished for that same closeness!

Each night as a child, I would pray to God to hear His voice in the same way they did. But there was only silence in return. Still, I kept praying that one day I would experience that same strong bond with God that the saints of old had attained.

As I grew into adulthood, I continued to pray and ask God for direction in my life. There was no doubt in my mind that He did hear and answer my prayers. That didn't mean I always got a green light for my desires and wants. Sometimes the answer was a resounding no, such as not getting a job I had wanted when I was unemployed. However, weeks later another job opportunity occurred that took care of our needs better. Without a doubt, this blessing was God's doing.

Other times my prayers were answered in the affirmative, such as when God led me to the right husband. It was a wonderful day when we got married in our local church. With family and friends taking part in the ceremony, I felt God's presence with us, blessing our union.

Still, I wondered if I would ever hear God speak to me in a more direct way, as the saints had in the stories I remembered from my childhood.

Daily I kept reading my Bible and praying for a closer relationship with God. I continued to wait and listen for His response. Then one day when I wasn't asking for God's direction and guidance, I received a special blessing from Him that I will cherish for the rest of my life.

It all began on one ordinary Monday evening. My husband and I had recently relocated to California for his job. Our home had a bicycle trail nearby that was full of wonderful scents from flowers and budding fruit trees. Since my husband was away at a seminar, I decided to go for a ride. I always felt close to God when I had the chance to see the beauty of nature. After returning home, I felt energized and thankful for all my blessings.

As I was preparing dinner for myself, my mother called from Virginia. "Your dad is in the hospital. The doctor said he's doing fine, but he wants to keep him overnight for observation."

"What happened to him?" I held my breath, fearful of the response.

"He was having some chest pains, so we thought it best to go to the hospital. But the doctor said it wasn't a heart attack."

His first heart attack had been eight years earlier, and he'd had another one five years after that. Whenever he had chest pains, a visit to the hospital was the natural course of action. In the past, he had been discharged from the hospital after the doctor's evaluation and EKG test. I hoped for the same results again.

Dad had come to value his health since that first heart attack and had learned to take better care of himself with more exercise and an improved diet plan. He'd told Mom, "God gave me extra time and I want to make the most of it." His checkup the previous month had showed he was doing fine. Still, anytime he would have chest pains, it gave Mom and the family cause for concern and extra prayers.

"Would you give him a call to lift his spirits? You know he doesn't like being in the hospital."

After she gave me the hospital's number, I promised to say some prayers for Dad and give him a call. The tone in my mother's voice made me believe there wasn't anything to be overly concerned about. He'd done these overnight stays before, and though it was a bit unnerving, it had come to be routine.

The chat with my dad was light and easy. He joked about the terrible hospital food and how he hoped to get in a game of golf the next day. That was his favorite form of exercise these days. His spirit was upbeat and cheerful. If my mother hadn't told me he was in the hospital, I would have thought he was relaxing in his favorite chair at home. As usual, I ended the call by saying, "I love you, Dad."

Though I was married and had my own home, I was still Daddy's little girl. I loved talking to him and getting his advice about work and our plans for the future. After the call, there was no thought in my mind that he wouldn't return home the following day. I started planning what we would do when my mom and dad came to visit in the next couple of months. I looked forward to showing off our new home and our favorite places to go.

Then it hit me like a lightning bolt. That small yet powerful voice of God spoke to my heart and told me that my dad was going to die. It was a voice that I had longed to hear, but not with this devastating news. Like the mere human that I am, I tried to argue with God in my spirit.

"This isn't his time yet. He's just retired," I pleaded.

Yet the response I heard was "It's my time."

Again I argued, "But he hasn't accomplished all he needs to do. He's hardly gotten to know his grandchildren."

"He's completed all he needs to do" was the resounding response.

I could tell my arguing was futile and going nowhere with God. Breaking down in tears, I prayed for acceptance and understanding.

The next day came and I went about my chores and work as usual. Though I felt blessed with the closeness I'd experienced with God the day before, I hoped the phrase "a day to

God is like a thousand years" (see Psalm 90:4) was a reality. I wanted many more years with my dad. Yet God was true to His word.

My brother called with the news that evening. He told me Dad had died of a heart attack earlier in the day.

Waves of emotion swept over me. I was heartbroken that he had died because I would no longer be able to talk to him and would miss him greatly. I was happy because I had made that final phone call and had one last opportunity to tell my dad how much I cared about him. But more than anything else, I was at peace in recalling God's prompting from yesterday and knew without a doubt my dad was in heaven with Him.

At the funeral, when we celebrated Dad's life and his walk with God, I continued to feel a peace that truly passes human understanding. God had prepared me for Dad's death and reminded me of his eternal life. I remembered my dad's words from our final phone call. He said, "You know, honey, I'm really looking forward to leaving the hospital and going home." This memory made me smile. You see, he got that final wish. He was at home in heaven!

Multiplying the Strength He Gave Me

ANNETTE M. ECKART

When the odd pains started I didn't really notice them because my father had just died and I had other things to worry about. The vague pains would come and go in my feet, my knees, and sometimes my hands.

Since I was busy with my husband, Ed, home, church involvement, and career demands as a manager for a Wall Street firm, it was easy for me to push the strange aches from my mind. And of course on top of all of that, I was preoccupied with my own grief and supporting my bereaved mother. My schedule could not accommodate imagined twinges in my body.

131

One Friday Mom spent the night with us, and the next day my sister-in-law, Karen, joined us for a shopping trip to the mall. Karen, a lively conversationalist, sat in the backseat and made us laugh. But I paused my listening and shifted my attention to driving my Honda when I approached a notoriously dangerous intersection where twelve lanes of traffic converged.

The traffic light turned red. Of course when lights turn red, we stop. But my foot physically wouldn't move to the brake!

Sounds of Karen and Mom laughing, cars whooshing past, and everything else faded around me. My eyes widened as the intersection loomed ahead. My heart raced.

Finally, my foot moved, but I had to press all of my 116 pounds against the pedal, bracing my hands on the wheel, to make up for lost time. Karen and Mom chatted, oblivious to what was happening.

The car stopped on the white line. I sat motionless, my eyes riveted on the red light while my brain whirred and tried to make sense of what had happened. Two of the most precious people in my world were in my car. They didn't know how close we had come to disaster.

The rest of the ride home was without incident, but I knew something was not right. And I knew it was time to deal with the twinges. The following Monday, I phoned my doctor.

At thirty-four years old and with some medical background, I knew I was in the perfect age group for the onset of multiple sclerosis. When Ed and I visited my doctor, I had already considered some of the worst-case scenarios. After examining me and asking questions, Dr. Sinha said, "I suspect arthritis. I would like you to see a rheumatologist."

Relief flooded me—all tension drained away.

Arthritis, is that all? I thanked God.

I had seen commercials for arthritis medicine. The gray-haired lady had trouble gardening and then took two pain-relieving pills. Thirty seconds later she happily dug her trowel into the soil, free of any limitation.

Everyone gets a touch of arthritis sooner or later. No problem, I thought.

I was about to find out how wrong I was.

Rheumatology appointments cluttered my calendar as we experimented with medications to relieve the weakness and the increasing symptoms of pain.

I had to ask Ed to help me more and more because I could no longer open jars, milk cartons, or medication bottles. I joined an American Arthritis Foundation support group as the disease progressed. I was the youngest person in the group, and I learned alarming facts.

Dr. Hayes Wilson, medical adviser to the Arthritis Foundation and director of rheumatology at Piedmont Hospital in Atlanta, calls rheumatoid arthritis a "very important and deadly disease. . . . It's not just 'take two aspirin and call me in the morning,'" he said. "Get an early diagnosis and treat it aggressively. The consequence of not treating it aggressively could be . . . mortality. We need to find out why it's killing people."[1]

Even though opinions differed on how to treat arthritis, everyone seemed to agree on one old adage: "Use it or lose it."

1. Carolyn Colwell, "Rheumatoid Arthritis Death Rate Unchanged," *HealthDay,* http://consumer.healthday.com/senior-citizen-information-31/misc-aging-news-10/ rheumatoid-arthritis-death-rate-unchanged-609491.html.

I was committed to being as active as possible. I could still be somewhat active in my field, though my income declined and my future looked dim.

The arthritis spread through my body like a growing tree. Beginning in my feet, it then affected my knees and my hips. It soon spread into my arms and hands. Arthritis can even affect eyes. Tough stuff for a thirty-four-year-old to deal with.

Our once-broad social circle began to shrink as I could participate in fewer activities. Ed and I loved sailing, but I could no longer hold nautical ropes. Sunset jeep drives on the beach or tent camping on the seashore ended because I couldn't tolerate the ride. We both had green thumbs, but our gardens fell into neglect.

Ed and I had hosted frequent dinner parties, preparing meals together and experimenting with new recipes. Now Ed took on more household responsibilities, and meals were simpler.

I had grown up winning dance contests and had regularly organized weekend dance parties with our friends, but now I couldn't get high heels on my painful feet. In fact, my feet were always heavy. As I walked, I started having to prompt myself: *I took two steps; I can take three. I took three; I can take four. . . .*

We rarely accepted invitations to events, but there was an exception. Our old friend Tom was marrying, and we wanted to be part of his celebration.

"I can't make the church and the reception. What should we do?" I asked Ed.

"Why don't we get there right before dinner, see them cut the cake, and send them off?" he suggested.

The day finally came. Ed drove the hour to the reception while I reclined my seat all the way back. Though it was early afternoon, I slept through the entire ride, thanks to the exhaustion of arthritis.

"We're here." Ed gently woke me. We walked to the hall, and when Ed opened the door, a flight of stairs faced us. How would I ever get up the staircase? I took a deep breath and slowly began the climb, using my hands to lift my right leg. I was exhausted when I reached the top. The disco music pounded, but Ed put his arm around my waist and drew me to a quiet corner before we entered the room.

"Okay, dearest?" I met his eyes, put the struggle behind me, and looked to a good evening.

Ed found our appointed table, and friends rushed over to hug us. Their loving concern brought tears to my eyes, but I also feared someone would squeeze me too tightly and hurt me.

The groom gave us a spectacular welcome. Then his bride told me, "Too bad you missed the wedding."

I felt the heat of humiliation and self-accusation. Because of *my* inability, we had missed their important moment.

The DJ spun "Cherish," and I shuffled onto the dance floor with Ed. He took me in his arms, I leaned against him, and we swayed, standing in the same spot. We left the event before finishing dinner. My mouth was dry from medication, I had no appetite, and my pain was building.

"Deteriorating."

"Inoperable."

"Incurable."

"Learn to live with the pain."

135

The diagnoses and the prognosis left me without hope. We had heard through church friends that a man named Reverend Kelleher, who had a healing ministry, was coming to our area. Ed and I decided to attend his healing service in a school auditorium.

We intentionally arrived late and sat in the last row because I knew I wouldn't have strength for the whole service, and we could then slip out unobtrusively. Hundreds of people were there. When people were invited forward for healing prayer, I hesitated. Ed looked at me, and I took courage because his heart was in his eyes. We walked down the aisle hand in hand.

An usher guided us to a man wearing a brown Franciscan habit, rope around his waist, and sandals on his feet. He asked us to tell him about my problem, and after listening to us he said, "A friend of mine had arthritis. He had healing prayer. That summer he started to improve, and by the end of the summer he was healed."

Reverend Kelleher put his hand on my shoulder and began to pray for my healing in Jesus' name. I left the auditorium, dragging my leg behind me, the same way I had come in.

But within a week I noticed a small yet significant change.

One morning, as I poured cereal into a bowl, I knew something was different. Hope sprang up. From that day, I began to improve. Stamina and physical ability increased.

Just as spring in New York causes the sap to run up in the trees and new buds to shoot forth, my strength began to return. My hands began to grip and twist off lids, to tug at the closures of stubborn juice containers and triumph over them. My feet became capable. I stopped counting my steps. And we began to reduce the medication. As the dosage decreased, my body health continued to increase.

The doctor had never seen anyone wean off the medication. Usually patients need additional drugs. Eight months later I was off all of my prescription medication and totally healed!

Ed and I looked for healing passages in the Bible. We read books written by Christians who prayed for the sick in Jesus' name and saw them healed. And then we began to pray for the sick in the prayer meeting we attended.

A woman with heel spurs received total relief when Ed prayed for her in Jesus' name. A man was relieved of back pain. A woman who couldn't lift her arm because of a rotator cuff problem was healed and cancelled her surgery.

People heard about what God was doing and sought us for healing prayer. After church on Sunday, people would surround us, asking for prayer. My hands had been aching and nearly useless months earlier, but now I felt the electricity of the Holy Spirit move through my fingers, sometimes all night long.

We continued to pray and study God's Word. Eventually, we both sensed the Lord prompting us to leave our careers. We began a ministry of healing through Jesus Christ called Bridge for Peace. We have ministered in twenty nations, teaching about Jesus Christ our Healer, praying for the sick, raising teams to pray for healing, and witnessing miracles.

While we were in Australia, a woman told me, "Annette, I almost called you. My nephew died three months ago from arthritis."

She fell sobbing into my arms. Without the power of Jesus Christ, I may well have shared the young man's story. The tragedy of his early death strengthened my resolve to push forward with a message of hope, and I determined anew to use the strength I've been given to help those who grope in the darkness of sickness and despair.

A Boatload of Trouble

Judy Parrott

Dad scrounged around for a hunk of wire to tie up the Buick's dilapidated muffler, found an illegal license plate for the trailer, and plugged the trailer's brake line into the car. However, he didn't tell me the only trailer he had to carry the twenty-seven-foot houseboat was way below capacity to haul this enormous burden. Dad also forgot to advise me to tighten the wheels' lug nuts every hundred miles during our trip from Michigan to Georgia.

What tiny wheels, I noticed, but never considered why.

My dad was a forgetful but lovable businessman who often took chances conservative people would never consider—especially this one: gambling with our very lives for the sake of a boat sale. Usually his risky decisions turned out all right, but this time I may not have been here to tell the story if God had been hard of hearing.

I took off that hot July day with my twelve-year-old son, Rob. I had never pulled such a giant boat before, but was impressed that Dad trusted me with his treasure.

We had a pleasant first night in the elegant new houseboat, parked in a Kentucky RV park. After breakfast, we headed to the Tennessee mountains. The trailer was struggling to stay straight behind the car.

Maybe I'm oversteering. I have to relax a bit, I thought.

The Buick had a hard time climbing the first high mountain. We finally got to the top, but trying to keep control as the boat shoved the car down the steep slope was another story.

The car and houseboat went faster and faster.

I pumped the brakes—no luck.

I smelled rubber and frantically scanned for an escape ramp, where trucks can coast upward off the road when they can't slow down.

But then it got worse!

With horror, I realized I'd lost control. The car began bucking and swaying across the four-lane highway. Then it headed for a ravine.

Rob was too scared to speak, sure we'd go over a cliff and die.

"Jesus!" I screamed at the top of my lungs.

Suddenly, as if it were shoved by some gigantic hand, the car spun completely around toward the median, and some large object flew over the hood.

Fifty feet of car and trailer abruptly stopped, spanning the entire highway.

Rob and I braced for the inevitable crash as vehicles flew around the curve at us.

The car stalled, but incredibly it started just in time to drag the trailer to the median, inches from traffic.

The boat loomed in the air like a sheltered queen on her throne, untouched. The only immediate visible damage was a badly twisted trailer hitch. We didn't yet realize the trailer axle had cracked almost in half, and the flying object was a tire.

A trucker, expecting a wreck, stopped nearby.

"I saw the wheels wobbling, and I knew you were in trouble," he said. The kind man separated my car from the trailer and handed me the twisted hitch parts. Rob and I headed for the nearest town.

I called my husband from a gas station in Lake City, Tennessee, and a stranger who heard our conversation offered to weld my broken hitch at no charge. A policeman in the gas station warned, "You are required to place triangular warning reflectors around that trailer or you will be responsible for any accidents it may cause."

Rob and I went shopping for reflectors, but the two hardware stores we found would not take a credit card, and I didn't have much cash.

Walk around the block, a voice nudged. A sign in a store window advertised the same reflectors on sale for *exactly* the amount of cash Rob and I had pooled together—nineteen whole dollars and eight cents. The Shepherd who promised to lead us had been there ahead of us, leveling our path.

After setting the warning signs around the boat, I went to town and called my dad. He felt guilty when I told him what had happened.

"It's all right, Dad," I said. "All's well that ends well."

But it wasn't over yet.

"Mom, there's a motel pool with a slide. Can we stay there and wait for Dad?" Rob asked.

After all the trauma I was happy to settle somewhere, have a nice dinner, and swim while we waited for my husband to arrive and help us finish taking the houseboat home. To top it all off, God painted us a picture: a magnificent peachy-gold sunset framed by craggy mountains.

What a way to end a supernatural day of deliverance from certain destruction!

In the meantime, after many phone calls, my husband, Roger, finally located an axle two hundred miles south of our Alpharetta, Georgia, home. The unusual-sized axle we needed was being tooled right then and would be finished by the time someone arrived. What was the chance of that?

Our son Dave, who lived near our home, offered to pick it up with his van. He arrived back at our house at 2 a.m. Then my husband got behind the wheel of Dave's van and took off in the night for Tennessee.

Not until he arrived in Lake City at 6 a.m. did Roger realize Dave hadn't given him the gas cap key. He had to take apart the pipe leading to the gas tank to fill it.

I was jarred awake early by a knock on the motel door, but was very thankful to see my weary husband. We drove the few miles to the highway to check out the boat and trailer.

It was gone! Not a sign of it anywhere!

I couldn't believe my eyes. I knew where I'd left it, but Roger thought I was confused.

"How could anyone move it with a cracked axle and no tire?" he asked.

We drove back to Lake City and asked a gas station attendant if he had seen a huge boat on the side of the road while driving to work. A woman walking by overheard us and said she had seen one being towed up the highway at 8 p.m. the evening before by Brown's Wrecking Company in nearby Clinton, Tennessee. She gave us directions, and we found it just where she had said.

We learned from Mr. Brown of the wrecking company that the police had ordered him to haul the hazard off the highway, so he had taken it to his shop. We were relieved to have a safe, level parking area in which to repair the trailer. Mr. Brown charged us a fair towing fee and even loaned us his tools—which mechanics tell me never happens.

While Roger tore the trailer apart to replace the axle, Mr. Brown directed me on my search for a bearing, a race, and two tires, since a second of the four had also been destroyed. The tires were a unique size, and not one was available within fifty miles. I stopped at a junkyard, my last hope, but to no avail.

Sitting on a pile of tires to call places farther away, I asked the Lord what to do.

Just then the clerk yelled, "Wow! Can you believe this? Lady, you are sitting on the very tires you need!"

He sold me two brand-new tires for only ten dollars. I often pondered how rare-sized, new tires came to be in a junkyard.

I finally located a bearing and other items at a parts store.

When I returned, I was upset to find that the bearing wasn't in the bag. Roger examined the wheel and realized he hadn't needed one after all; I was relieved to find the parts store had not charged me for it. That again confirmed God's invisible presence, and it thrilled me to know He was so involved in every detail.

Before sundown the new axle was in place, so Roger and Rob took off with the car and trailer. Roger had not been able to repair the trailer brakes, so I was concerned about his driving through the mountains.

"Please sleep in the boat overnight and fix them tomorrow," I pleaded.

He insisted they would be fine and was determined to be home by midnight. At least the lug nuts were tight, but the trailer was no sturdier than before. Off they went, with me following in the van, praying fervently.

They climbed the first steep mountain, but on the descent the car started fishtailing.

I watched in horror. They were soon out of control, just as I had feared, heading for a steel rail.

Beyond the rail was a huge chunk of nothing!

I screamed for Jesus again, and in an instant, they stopped wobbling and straightened out as if nothing had happened.

I didn't know how Roger felt, but I was trembling.

I pulled into the next rest area, turned off the engine, and wept. After a few moments, I turned the key to start the car, but nothing happened.

I was flabbergasted. The battery was dead.

Everyone at the rest area noticed when I opened the hood, and they surrounded me, trying to help. Nothing they tried worked.

Then I thought about all the miracles I had experienced earlier that day. I stood amid my new companions and asked God to start the van.

I slammed the hood shut, got back in, turned the key, and away I flew, like Elijah in the chariot!

The people who'd offered to help me stood there staring at my rear window. That would have been a perfect time for an altar call!

Soon I noticed that my gas was nearly gone.

"Lord," I prayed, "I have a problem here. I have no gas cap key and no cash. What do I do now?"

Follow that semitruck ahead of you, a voice inside said.

It immediately exited, and so did I. There in front of me loomed a gas station, though there had been no sign of one from the road. The attendant listened to my problem, reached into his pocket, and amazingly pulled out a gas cap key! He even accepted my credit card.

Finally entering our hometown, I stopped at a light. There went the boat across my path at the intersection, heading safely home.

These are only a few of the miracles God did on that trip. Whenever I am tempted to get discouraged, I remember what He has done for me in the past. The list is long and still growing. He promised to work all things out for good for those who love Him, and He does.

A Guy Named Andy

TIMOTHY J. BURT

I was walking past the Denver Mint on a nearly perfect evening in early September. I had just eaten my one meal of the day at a local burger place and was casually wandering back to the Episcopal church where I had stayed in the basement the previous three nights with other street people, indigents, and runaways.

At nineteen years old, I'd left home one night near the end of August and hitchhiked from Monmouth County, New Jersey, to Denver, Colorado. I'd had enough of the long history of constant turmoil, criticism, and abuse in my family. The problems had escalated that summer after my younger brother flunked out of college because of his partying and drug use. Not only was Bob using, but my folks also discovered he was dealing numerous drugs.

Unfortunately, according to my atheist father, my giving my life to Jesus that summer was equally disturbing. He made it clear that his hopes and dreams for both my brother and me were shattered.

One night I simply could take no more and escaped. With fifty dollars in my pocket, a sleeping bag, and my backpack full of clothes and snacks, I left for Colorado at 2:30 a.m. I planned to go to Steamboat Springs and be a ski bum.

God had other plans.

A stranger approached me in front of the Denver Mint.

"Hi, there," I said.

"And how are you this evening, my brother?" he responded.

Within moments he correctly assessed that I'd not had much to eat that day, and he insisted that I go with him to get some food. I resisted but he insisted.

His name was Andy Witherspoon, and he told me that he worked construction in the Denver area and that he spent a lot of time helping street kids and runaways. He said he lived outside of town somewhere and that, since he gave away most of the money he made, everything he owned was in the modest gym bag he carried.

Andy was a short, slight, middle-aged black man, and I wondered how he was able to handle construction.

Andy seemed to intuitively know a lot about me, but I guessed since he spent a lot of time with runaways, there must be some commonality. He understood my discomfort with the contrast between my abusive home situation and my newfound faith, and he did not condemn me for leaving, but he was concerned about the distance I'd come and the resentments I harbored.

While we ate, he suggested that I go home and reconcile with my parents. This little man who had never finished ninth grade strongly recommended continuing my college education, even though I didn't see the point—in my opinion, the Lord was coming back within a few years.

Godly wisdom and counsel poured from this humble little man, but I was too hardened to receive it.

Night fell and Andy instructed me to watch how he dealt with a panhandler. Only six or seven minutes later he sent the man away without what he thought he needed: money. Instead, Andy spoke respectfully into the man's heart and addressed his real need, which was spiritual. The man walked away smiling after only a few minutes of interaction with Andy Witherspoon. Such was the wisdom and love this man exuded.

Then Andy and I met a rich kid from Indiana who was physically disabled. The kid was living in an expensive Denver hotel. Andy treated this rich kid with the same respect and dignity he'd shown the panhandler thirty minutes before. I realized that none of my professors at college had the wisdom or knowledge of this gentle man. No one I'd ever met spoke like Andy Witherspoon.

He suggested that the guy from Indiana let me stay in his hotel room for the night, and the guy agreed. I didn't need to go back to the Episcopal church, since everything I owned was on my back. I appreciated a clean, safe, quiet room that night and never thought I'd see Andy again.

The next morning I awoke and left the hotel early. Two days before, I'd helped a couple of young pastors move some equipment and theatrical lighting. They had invited me to a special Sunday morning musical at the First Church of the Nazarene, and I was determined to get there. I had hitch-hiked over 1,500 miles in the last week, and now, while I was hitchhiking to a church only seven miles away on a Sunday morning, the police found me, ticketed me, and got me to the church on time. The only ticket I got during my whole trip was in Denver, trying to get to church.

I enjoyed the production and was invited to stay for the potluck lunch afterward. Afterward, one of the families at the potluck dropped me off near the bus station. I planned to take the next bus to Steamboat Springs and do my ski-bum thing.

But God had other plans.

Because I'd gone to church that morning, I'd missed the early bus to Steamboat. The next bus didn't leave until Sunday night. I suddenly had lots of time to explore or just relax on another perfect afternoon in early September.

I stretched out on the grass in the middle of Denver's largest park and closed my eyes. I didn't even look up when I thought I heard my name because, after all, no one knew me and I was all alone in this huge park.

The voice again clearly called "Tim!" and I sat up and looked around. It was Andy Witherspoon! He had not been there when I'd lain down only two or three minutes earlier. I told him all about the church musical, getting a ticket from the police, my plans for Steamboat, the schedule for the next bus, and what I thought my future would look like.

This time while we talked, I insisted that he go with me for something to eat—my treat this time. We found a local chicken place and sat together talking again.

"What a coincidence that I happened to lie down in the park at the same time you were there. . . ."

Yeah, some "coincidence."

Andy did all he could to convince me to go home. He said two wrongs didn't make a right; and he told me again to go home, be reconciled with my parents, and return to school. He told me not to worry about what courses I took or what kind of grades I got, just to go to college to learn *how* to learn. And this from a man who said he never finished ninth grade.

His words hit me hard. Truth was having an impact. God broke me right there, right then. I couldn't stop crying, sitting in a public eatery with a short, middle-aged man. I kept turning my face toward the wall as Andy's wisdom and care challenged my plans and assuaged nearly twenty years of hurts and fears and criticism.

Andy knew that the ski-bum lifestyle would take me away from my newfound faith in God. He also knew that I had not received God's message the previous night. I told Andy I would not go to Steamboat—I would head home.

We must have said good-bye after finishing our meal, but all these years later I simply can't remember. Instead of the 7:30 p.m. bus to Steamboat, I bought a ticket to Omaha, Nebraska—as far as I could go on my remaining money.

Who was Andy Witherspoon? He just "happened" to appear at two critical points in this journey with guidance from God specifically for me, and he claimed to live outside of Denver someplace. But he had no car to get back and forth, and he claimed to have only one change of clothes and a few incidentals in his gym bag. Andy claimed to work in the construction industry, which is usually reserved for rough-and-tumble guys who are not Andy's diminutive size and don't possess his gentle character. And he gave away most of his money?

I'm reminded of Hebrews 13:2: "Don't forget to show hospitality to strangers, for some who have done this have entertained angels without realizing it!"

It was 11:30 p.m. in Omaha, and I began hitchhiking, headed east. A guy in his thirties picked me up in his little sports car. He was going to Illinois and said he could use the company to help him stay awake. He also could use some gas—his fuel gauge indicated his tank was less than a quarter full. We started looking for gas as we left downtown Omaha and even pulled off the highway a couple times, only to find the gas stations closed. The stranger and I drove all night, until nearly 6 a.m., before we found a gas station that was about to open.

There was no earthly way we could've driven that long on a quarter tank of gas. God had multiplied the fuel—it was clearly a miracle!

I hitchhiked the rest of the way home and finished college and played in a Christian band. The life journey God arranged for me ultimately led to graduate school, a vocation as a Christian counselor, and volunteering as a hospital chaplain. I feel privileged to be involved in these ministries and to know that God is using me to influence others—in a small way—as Andy impacted me so long ago.

The Scent of Blessing

Deb Wuethrich

If you've ever been on a merry-go-round, you'll understand the whirling, twirling sensation that results from spinning in circles too fast. When your brain's electrochemistry goes awry, the vertigo is not unlike that merry-go-round ride, leaving you dizzy, dazed, and disoriented.

Add a personal encounter with demons and the need to do spiritual battle—spiritual warfare—and it's a wild ride. My story of just such a ride may sound bizarre, but it's true.

Whenever I heard of someone hearing voices, I pictured a person who'd pretty much lost it as far as relating in the real world. I envisioned someone probably living on the street.

If a person was said to be battling demons, I didn't think of it as a literal war. To me, angels were all positive beings of light; I never considered some could be the dark, fallen spirits I'd only read about or seen in scary movies. These were beliefs I held—until these experiences happened to me.

One day I heard voices, and they weren't nice ones at all. They were vile and vicious, all too eager to point out and remind me of my failures—continually. I felt I'd met spirits that weren't in any way angelic but only temporarily posing as beings of light when I first encountered them. They were actually on the opposing team, assigned to keep me off guard, depressed, and discouraged.

The battle that raged within was a spiritual one with forces that pulled and warred with my soul. It was a palpable thing, with such agitation I felt like I was continually on an out-of-control merry-go-round I couldn't get off, spinning in a vortex that wouldn't release its hold. It was exhausting.

One day the war escalated. I not only heard voices but also sensed an imposing dark spirit in the room with me. I couldn't see it, but that made it no less real as its voice taunted me.

"God came like a thief in the night, but you weren't ready," the voice announced. "He has abandoned you, and He's never coming back."

The dark spirit terrified me. I wanted an exorcist!

What I got was a trip to the emergency room, hallucinating as my panic-stricken husband folded me into the car as fast as he could. There, they diagnosed the condition as a mild form of a mental illness, but the unceasing commentary in my head droned on for weeks.

Strangely, the scenarios laid out before me were of a religious nature, leaving doubts and questions weighing heavily upon my soul. I soon recognized this battle being waged as something I'd only read about—spiritual warfare.

Sadly, most medical practitioners believe only in the physiological causes of such a state, and my doctors were no exception. They weren't interested in exploring the spiritual implications of what I was experiencing, so I was left to deal with it myself.

Just prior to these odd occurrences, I'd owned up to the fact that I'd been traveling a wretched road. In fact, my life had nearly derailed, and deep rifts had formed in my relationship with my husband. I recall asking God's forgiveness for a long spell of wrong living, bad habits, and atrocious behaviors.

I wanted help turning things around. Having spent too much time in messy places, I hoped it wasn't too late. I wanted forgiveness and new direction, but I guess the Evil One didn't like that and refused to let go without a fight.

To make matters even worse, I'd tried a New Age solution to my problems. I'd recently allowed a psychic to do an "angel reading" to learn the names of the heavenly beings that she said could help me. The trouble came when that encounter opened the door to another sort of being—those dark spirits who taunted me day and night, but especially in the darkness as I curled up in the fetal position on my bed.

"Tonight is the end of the world," said a voice slithering through the darkness. "Don't worry. You aren't going to die. You're going to live forever—in torment! You don't deserve anything better."

I was forced to listen to my worthlessness as a person because there was no way to shut off the voices. Demons rolled out my unworthiness as a child of God before me like scenes from a horror movie, mistake by detailed mistake.

"Your husband is going to leave you and there's no way back," the voice continued.

Oddly, a sneering demon voice asked me relentless questions regarding things I'd heard from the Bible.

"Do you know of the woman on the creature's back?" the voice asked. "The Bible says, 'They will eat her flesh and burn her with fire' (Revelation 17:16 NIV). That is *your* fate. The woman is you."

The words sounded convincing, but I didn't really know if they were true because I hadn't read my Bible in a long time.

Then one day after cowering and covering my ears—and waiting for medical science to kick in through medication that was supposed to somehow balance my brain's whacked-out electrochemistry—I felt the urge to begin reading my Bible in earnest. Once I opened it, I couldn't stop and embarked on a mad, obsessive crash course through its pages.

I could see the demon voice was presenting twists and half-truths directly from the Scriptures. But then something extraordinary happened, something comforting, right in the midst of turmoil. Another voice—a still, small one—coaxed, "Go deeper."

And I did.

He added, "Do not be afraid, for I am with you. Always."

Soon I came across the passage that had been described. It was in Revelation 17. There was indeed a beast and a sinful woman, but God showed me that the passage was allegorical, and the "woman" referred to a great city ruling over kings of the earth. I read the passage in context and was learning to discern the truth—that true believers would always go with God.

So the dark spirit changed tactics. Sometimes I'd *smell* his presence. Unbidden thoughts that I perceived as a voice said things to me such as, "Just wait until you see what I have in store for you," and within minutes I'd smell the stench of a skunk outside my window.

Occasionally I smelled smoke that no one else could smell. The worst was when I smelled the sickly odor of sulfur, and I pictured the lake of fire.

"That's for you," the demon voice taunted. And I shuddered.

I remember the day I sat in my study, reading God's Word, and my mind drifted off to the pull of the singsong voice, which was now in the background thanks to medication, but could still be an incessant annoyance.

All of a sudden, I noticed a very pleasant aroma. I looked around and saw a small candle on a nearby shelf. I picked it up and read the label on the bottom, which said the scent was "Blessing." It was made from frankincense, cedar wood, and lemon, and it made me think of the "aroma of Christ" I'd read about and the "fragrance of the knowledge of him" found in 2 Corinthians 2:14 (ESV).

It also reminded me of Mary's anointing of Jesus with expensive perfume just a short time before His death. Around Easter that year, I heard a radio personality talk about how Jesus must have carried that scent with Him, even as He led the Last Supper. The disciples would have picked up the lingering aroma, even as He washed their feet. Judas would have smelled it then and as he pointed Him out in the Garden of Gethsemane. It was possibly lingering faintly in the air as soldiers beat Him.

The scent of the candle made me think of Him, and I felt good. It helped counter the offensiveness I'd just experienced when the taunting threatened to break through once again.

As weeks passed, the voices in my head lessened. Medical science did its part, but I believe God was also teaching me to discern in a spiritual way, encouraging a reaction of faith and not fear whenever I had to face things in the supernatural realm. He taught me to cope in the physical world as He began to heal my faltering marriage through my husband's tender attentiveness during this odd mental health journey.

One day, however, I was in the newsroom where I work. Without warning, I smelled smoke and sulfur. No one else seemed to notice. It can be lonely suffering a spiritual affliction when those around you can't.

With the bad smells came a catapult of negative thoughts and anxiety as I recalled some of what I'd been through the past few months, and I feared a relapse.

Shortly after the invisible thrust and parry in the spiritual realm, the air around me suddenly changed. I smelled incense—a scent not unlike my candle that was still at home. It was as if someone had moved through the air in front of me, the way an anointed person might leave a cloud of cologne or perfume in his or her wake, or a signature fragrance.

Peace replaced my distress. At that very moment, I knew beyond doubt that Jesus was there with me in that room. It was true what the Bible said: God always leads in triumphal procession (2 Corinthians 2:14), as the same passage about His fragrance notes. And it is He, not I, who will do the battle, for as soon as I caught the scent of blessing, the offensive smells immediately evaporated.

Sometimes even now I will catch the smell of real smoke or something nasty like sulfur and recall those odd times of affliction. They say olfactory experience is one of the strongest senses for memory. I will sometimes pick up my Blessing candle and deliberately enjoy its scent, recalling that extraordinary time when God let me know that I was not alone to fight a skirmish in the battle of spiritual warfare. He was right where He promised He'd be—with me, always.

Nothing Is Incurable

MARTY PRUDHOMME

F ibromyalgia is incurable, and we do not know what causes it. You will probably be confined to a wheelchair as you grow older," the doctor explained.

At the time, only pain pills and muscle relaxers were available to treat fibromyalgia. Dr. Samuel did not believe they were the answer, since they were addictive and I would need increasingly stronger doses to control the pain.

He did give me a prescription to help me sleep and sent me to a physical therapist who specialized in fibromyalgia. The doctor said physical therapy would ease some of the stiffness and keep my muscles moving longer.

After twenty-five years of aches and pains, I was relieved to finally know what was wrong with me. As difficult as the diagnosis was, I was certainly relieved to know I was not a hypochondriac. In the past, doctors had treated my various symptoms without knowing what was causing the problems.

My struggle began in my late twenties when I noticed pain in my legs and feet. I thought it was poor circulation, so I wore heavy support hose, though it was certainly not fashionable for a young woman. When my shoulders began to ache, I assumed it was tension and was thankful for anyone who would rub my shoulders and neck.

Many faithful friends prayed for me, and those prayers sustained me through years of bursitis, knee pain, and other odd aches. For an entire year severe pain filled my rib cage—so sharp I would wonder if a rib was cracked or out of place. The doctor said it was costochondritis, inflammation in the rib cage, possibly from hormonal changes in my forties. I felt like a chronic complainer while the various aches and pains went on and on.

For many years I looked normal on the outside, so my family did not understand what I was going through. They complained, "You never want to do anything anymore!" because they didn't know that even walking hurt.

The physical therapist helped me keep moving, but on the days she did deep muscle massage we would both cry. She cried because she hurt me, and I cried because she hurt me. She assured me, "This is good for you; it will keep your muscles moving."

But my routine didn't change much. I lay on the sofa day after day watching dust bunnies float around while the laundry piled up. One day my husband threw several loads of laundry on top of me. Some of the towels were still warm from the dryer. I thought, *This is good. Just bury me in laundry; it's as good a way to go as any.*

Gradually, the stiffness began to overtake my muscles. I was fifty years old, but rigidity and pain caused me to walk like a person of eighty. Another side effect of the fibromyalgia was sleeplessness. I usually slept only two hours a night, so I could hardly function mentally or physically. The simplest tasks took tremendous time and effort.

I will never forget the afternoon I came home from a particularly difficult therapy session with my back, legs, and shoulders throbbing. I buried my face in the sofa cushion and wept.

"God, if you never heal me, if I never get off this sofa, I will still trust in you," I cried. "Even if the pain never goes away and I can't take care of my family, I know you are good. Nothing can separate me from your great love. You will never leave me, and I choose to put my trust in you."

A great calm came over me and I felt peace from deep within. I knew whatever the future held for me, God was on my side. It was a win-win situation. If God had plans for me to serve Him outside of my home, He would heal me. If He wanted me to stay on the sofa and trust Him, that's what I would do.

This was such a simple prayer of surrender, but I believe I turned a spiritual corner. I felt an overwhelming sense of well-being as the days passed. Nothing had changed physically; I was still in pain, but I knew everything would be all right.

A few months later I went to a ladies' retreat and talked with a woman I had not seen since the previous year's retreat. Bernita told me she had a dream in which she saw me bowed down, praying.

"Do you have fibromyalgia?" she asked. "In my dream I heard the Lord say He was healing you of fibromyalgia."

Bernita did not know me very well and had no idea of my struggle.

"What is fibromyalgia?" she asked. She knew nothing about the condition. I laughed because I knew her dream was sent from God. He was letting me know I would be healed. Bernita prayed for me that day, and I promised to let her know when God healed me.

Six months later I was still the same. Then my friend Gail invited me to visit her in Oregon. She said I needed a change of scenery and sent me an airline ticket. Gail and her husband, Greg, are ministers and had served as missionaries to Costa Rica, where they saw God heal many people through prayer. They had prayed for me many times, and they believed in miracles.

"We don't know what God will do. Just come and let us love on you," Gail said.

As I boarded the plane a sense of expectancy filled me.

The first evening I was there, Gail had a group of ladies at her house for a Bible study. After she finished teaching, Gail asked the ladies if they would like to pray for anything.

"I think we should pray for Marty," one lady said shyly.

They gathered around me and began to pray that the sickness in my body be bound and that healing be released in Jesus' name. I relaxed and felt the warmth of their hands on my shoulders. A sweet peace came over me.

After prayer, Gail served refreshments while we chatted. Half an hour later, I realized I could still feel the warmth of a hand on my shoulder. I did not feel any pain. I mentioned this sensation to the ladies, and we rejoiced that it was the touch of the Lord.

I knew God had healed me. Fireworks did not fill the skies or sound in my ears. I didn't hear a heavenly voice. I just knew God's peaceful assurance: I was healed! That night I went to sleep praising the Lord for His goodness and slept all night for the first time in years.

The next day we cleaned out Gail's kitchen cabinets. I was on the floor with my head in a cabinet when I noticed I had no pain. It was the first time since I was in my twenties that I had worked without hurting.

I spent a month in Oregon with my friends. We walked along the wildly beautiful Pacific Ocean beaches, hiked on trails in the lush Cascade Mountains, and climbed to see spectacular waterfalls. We laughed at anything and everything as the joy of the Lord bubbled from within us and overflowed. I felt like a bird released from its cage, like a captive set free from a prison cell.

That was fifteen years ago, and I'm still pain free. After twenty-five years of suffering, I am healed.

Fibromyalgia is not too difficult for God. He still performs signs and wonders today; He still heals the sick. Working miracles is what He does best.

A Critical Left Turn

TRISH PROPSON

B est week of my life!" My fourteen-year-old daughter, Alyssa, chattered from the passenger seat. We were returning decorations from the homeschool prom we had hosted the night before. She was still glowing from the memories of the wonderful experience with her friends. I was basking in the accomplishment of pulling off the most epic youth event of my life.

After our errand, we were going to tour a cosmetology school she was interested in attending after high school. Then she would travel with her friends to a youth retreat in the Wisconsin north woods. All was well in her world, and I was delighted to be sharing in her joy—feeling partially responsible for her happiness.

On top of everything else, it was a beautiful sunny day in Wisconsin. The sky was bright blue with a few wispy clouds. The air was cool and damp with the smell of spring chasing through the freshly plowed fields that surrounded us. We turned onto the country road near our home to get on the highway.

"What was your favorite part about the . . ."

I no sooner started my question when I saw a black truck cross the center line in front of us. I screamed. A voice screamed back, "Turn left."

I cranked the steering wheel as hard as I could just as we made impact. We were traveling fifty-five miles an hour, and the truck was easily doing the same.

I heard his engine revving, and all I saw was black as the truck rammed headfirst into our minivan and catapulted over the top of us.

I took my hands off the wheel, knowing I could do nothing but surrender my life into God's hands. As the van spun across the median and into a parking lot, I screamed Alyssa's name.

The van lurched to a stop. My first thought was that I shouldn't be alive. Frantic, I asked Alyssa if she was okay.

"I'm fine," she said calmly.

Knowing my daughter was alive and not critically injured, my second thought was sadness that I was alive. I could have been joining Jesus in heaven. I felt a kind of surreal betrayal overtake me as that thought swept through my heart.

"Get out of the van and call Dad," I commanded.

The vehicle was filling with smoke and I told her to run. I wrenched the driver's door open and fell to the pavement. The owner of the gas station parking lot we landed in ran to me.

"Are you okay?" His ashen face tightened with fear.

"Turn off the engine. It's on fire," I yelled.

With a puzzled look on his face, he complied. He grabbed my keys and brought them to me.

"You shouldn't be alive," he said with amazement.

Another witness came over to describe the accident. "I thought I saw three people die today. I can't believe you are alive." He was shaking.

Sitting on the asphalt with my head in my hands, I looked at the motionless driver in the mangled truck. He was slumped over with blood pouring from his head. Surely dead, but I lifted a prayer for him.

My son and husband arrived quickly since our home was three miles from the accident. Seeing that we were alive, my husband listened to the details from the witnesses and spoke with the first responders. Alyssa quietly asked if she would be able to go camping. I was dazed, trying to understand what had happened.

I asked my husband if the engine was on fire. He assured me the engine was not on fire. I realized the airbags must have been the source of the smoke I had seen. I went to the front of the vehicle to see for myself. I stopped and began to cry.

There was no engine. The space where our legs had been only minutes earlier protruded past where the engine had been mounted. The engine had been completely torn away, and the metal bars that surrounded our bodies hung into open air untouched. A trail of mangled metal and debris littered the scene with what had once been our engine.

I began to shake. The realization that God had spared our lives began to sink in.

The first responders attended to Alyssa. She was walking and talking. Bruises were beginning to show up on her neck and chest from the seat belt.

"I can't believe she's alive," a young firefighter exclaimed. My legs were badly swollen. Bruises were starting to appear on my legs, neck, and torso, too. I couldn't stand and I was pretty sure my arm was broken.

The only injuries we sustained were from the seat belts and airbags. With only one ambulance available, I rushed the responders to the other driver, who was alive but unconscious.

"You shouldn't be alive," the police officer said as he took my report.

"I've heard that a lot in the past few minutes," I replied with a weak smile.

"You know both vehicles were going over fifty-five miles an hour. There is no reason you are here right now," he said rather matter-of-factly. "If you hadn't hit him head on, we wouldn't be talking right now."

"Wait. What?" I asked.

"I don't know how you knew to turn into the crash. But if you hadn't turned left when you did, he would have hit you on the driver's side door. You would have died instantly and your daughter wouldn't be walking."

He finished his report as the reality of his words penetrated my soul. His partner went on to tell me that the Chrysler minivan we were driving was specifically designed to withstand high-speed, head-on collisions. If we had been in any other vehicle, or been hit in any other direction, we probably would not have survived the impact.

How did I know to turn left? It happened so fast. I didn't have time to do anything. Whose voice told me to turn left?

The emergency room doctors repeated the phrase we had heard many times that day: "You shouldn't be alive."

My daughter and I spent the next few months recovering from the accident—me with my battered neck, damaged shoulder, and broken arm; and her with a wounded neck and broken spine.

The words I heard in that moment right before impact often ran through my mind.

Turn left.

I came to rest in the truth that it had been God's voice guiding me into a second chance at His plans for my life. My daughter is alive and well and pursuing God's plan for her life.

I trust that my divine left turn was an audible instruction allowing me the chance to embrace the purpose and work God has for me now. And someday when it is my time to meet my Savior, I hope He will once again, at the exact moment, tell me to turn left. I can careen full speed through the gates of heaven, parts falling off in every direction, and roll to a stop to hear Him say, "Welcome home."

A New Creation

KELLY J. STIGLIANO

I could have been the poster child for bad choices.

I had lived with a pattern of poor decisions that had left me with stomach ulcers, colitis, and excessive acids in my gallbladder—all by the age of eighteen.

I was only eighteen the night the pain from my bad choices sent me to the emergency room.

After the tests were all done and I received the surprising diagnosis of just what was wrong with me, yet another shock was ahead. The doctor paused at the door. He looked over his shoulder and said, "Oh, and you *do* know you're pregnant, don't you?"

No, I had no idea I was pregnant. My wild lifestyle had finally caught up with me.

My life spun ahead at a breakneck pace. A quick wedding turned into a violent marriage, and we added a second baby. Slowly, I gathered courage to flee my abusive marriage.

Next thing I knew, I was the twenty-three-year-old single mom of two children.

But having children doesn't mean you've matured.

Working two jobs and partying left me little room to practice positive parenting. My excessive drinking exacerbated my intestinal issues.

A wake-up call should have come when the doctor refused to prescribe Tagamet for my conditions anymore. Instead, he insisted I change my lifestyle.

I didn't listen. Instead, Maalox became my best friend. I had a large bottle of it in my desk at work and one at home. I guzzled it like water.

Then God stepped in to save me from my self-destructive behavior.

Mark introduced himself to me on Live Rock-and-Roll Night at the Cosmopolitan, a club I frequented. I loved going there on Thursday nights because they featured rock music—a refreshing change from the disco scene everyone was into. I hated disco and lived for Thursdays out with my friend Sue.

While he wasn't living a life in keeping with his Christian heritage, Mark still had the path to God in his peripheral vision. We started going out and he invited me to go to church with him. Thanks to his family and their support, my two toddlers and I became faithful church attenders. In time, my relationship with Mark went by the wayside as I grew in my walk with God.

Even without Mark, the kids and I continued to attend church and Sunday school. We read the Bible and prayed together. I was amazed that my children were like little sponges, soaking up the love of Jesus and the Bible stories. I learned patience, respect, and kindness, becoming an attentive and loving mother to my children.

I was growing in my Christian walk and felt an overwhelming desire to put my daughter in Christian school as she reached kindergarten age. Although I was poor, in my new-found faith, I enrolled her in a small Christian school in the country. That's where I met her unmarried principal, Jerry Stigliano.

Sometimes secrets shared between two friends aren't meant to be kept private. As I told a friend that I had my eye on Mr. Stigliano, she had been trying to find a good husband for me and a good dad for my kids. She initiated her own "phone a friend" system, so Principal Stigliano soon learned of my interest in him.

He must have shared the interest, because Jerry asked me out, and we quickly became exclusive. My children loved him; he was so caring and patient with them. His interest in me and concern for our well-being warmed my heart.

One evening after we had been dating for a couple months, Jerry asked us over for dinner. He had made his specialty— spaghetti. It was delicious and we all ate our fill.

But I still suffered from colitis, and before long I knew I had to get home—fast.

As I hurriedly carried my sleeping children out to the car, Jerry said, "Have you ever asked God to heal your colitis?"

"No, I never thought about it."

"Well, you should ask Him," he said. "It's a problem from your old life. You're a new creation in Christ now. You should ask Him to take away this reminder of the past."

I shrugged.

"Just ask," he urged.

I looked at him and tilted my head sideways, thinking about what he'd said.

"Hmm. Okay," I responded with a nod. "I'll ask! Gotta go; talk to you later!"

As I drove home, the children slept in the backseat.

"He's right," I prayed out loud. "My colitis *is* from my old life. I *am* a new creation. God, would you please take away my colitis?"

A simple prayer from a baby Christian.

Almost instantly I felt warmth deep within my lower hips. By the time I arrived home my symptoms were gone. I've not suffered from colitis since that amazing night. I was healed, and all I had to do was ask!

I recently turned fifty and had my first colonoscopy since I was eighteen. An unexplained anemia also mandated an upper GI endoscopy at the same time. The scopes revealed that my insides are pink and healthy, with no scarring.

When I spoke to the doctor and read the reports, I smiled. I knew I had been healed years earlier, but it was just so nice to finally have a good report in writing!

Penniless in Bangkok

SCOTI SPRINGFIELD DOMEIJ

The pauper clutched a pulverized tin cup on his battered wheelchair's armrest. He resembled a stone Buddha perched stoically on his wheeled throne. Instead of knees, two stumps jutted out a few inches past his well-worn seat. Healed balls of skin capped his amputated stubs.

Each day for five days, I passed this beggar, who was surrounded by chaos. His back wheels were parked too near the curb's ledge, a hair's breadth from speeding cars almost shaving the back of his dilapidated wheelchair.

The sky train overhead sliced through the heat and humidity. Harried pedestrians swerved between the crowds packing the sidewalk, scrawny stray dogs, and speeding motorcycles that had jumped the curbs to escape traffic gridlock. A bouquet of garlic, ginger, and oil drifted from food carts. Trinket hawkers squawked at tourists.

Loose tiles, broken pavement, and sinkholes threatened to turn my ankles. How this disabled man navigated his wheelchair over cracks and gaping holes through the motorized and human congestion mystified me.

He was camouflaged by the urban landscape, and indifferent passersby hardly glanced at the beggar. I smiled, attempting to catch his eye. He focused straight ahead with a cold, blank stare.

I was on a tight budget, but I resolved to save all my loose coins to plunk in his cup before I left Thailand. Each time I ate a meal or shopped, I paid with only paper *baht*, the Thailand currency. My excitement rose as all of the change earmarked for the amputee weighed down my purse.

The morning of December 22, my last day in Bangkok, I calculated my agenda in fifteen-minute increments to avoid stress or any chance of missing my plane. My first priority? The beggar.

I caught the skytrain to the beggar's spot. My change clanked into his metal cup.

That's probably more money than he receives in a month.

His frigid eyes never blinked acknowledgment. Not one facial muscle communicated "thank you."

How many times had I taken God or others for granted when they provided small miracles?

I made a few more impulsive purchases and received more change. I saw the paraplegic teetered on the filthy curb's edge between the busy street and crowded sidewalk. He seemed alive only from the waist up, since his shriveled legs looked as lifeless as his ancient, soiled wooden crutches. I dropped all my coins into his cup and then remembered, *I have more.*

I burrowed deep into my purse, and my fingers scraped together more change. As the coins clinked into his cup, our gaze locked—two people from different worlds. His toothless smile and joyful eyes sparkled with thanks.

On my jaunt back to the hotel, my heart ached.

I wish I'd prayed, "In the name of Jesus, get up and walk!"

The truth is, I lacked the faith or the courage.

After returning to the hotel, I bargained hard with the taxi driver to avoid being overcharged for the ride to Bangkok International Airport. As we sped along the freeway, he said, "I miss my daughter. She live five hours away. To make money, I buy taxi and work in Bangkok. The cost of gas hurt my business."

From the debris littering his front seat, I suspected he ate and slept in his taxi. As a single mother, too often in the past I had worried I wouldn't have enough money to fill my tank with gas to drive to work.

By the time I recited my entire Thai vocabulary, we were nearly at the airport.

"You speak Thai good. How much you pay?"

"Just as we agreed, three hundred baht." His eyes blinked his disappointment. "You single woman. I take good care of you."

At the Bangkok International Airport, the taxi driver unloaded and stacked my slippery plastic luggage onto a baggage cart. I pressed all my currency into his hand—five hundred baht (about $16.50), plus eight American dollars. I was flat broke, but I didn't need any money until I returned home. The taxi driver's beaming smile made my heart dance.

We hugged. His soft check rubbed mine. I'd miss the "Land of the Smiles." The Thai people's gentle, hospitable nature made me wonder if they were God's angels on earth.

I dragged the unwieldy cart through the doors of the international departure building to my first checkpoint, the VAT (tourist value-added tax) desk.

The revenue officer stamped my VAT refund application. My boss had warned me that I had to pay an immigration exit tax before leaving Thailand, and I counted on the 1,400 baht ($46) VAT refund to pay that exit tax.

I waited for my cash refund only to be informed, "This is not the VAT refund counter." A slight spike of anxiety radiated from my chest to my throat.

After passing through security, I checked into China Airlines and received my boarding pass. The beautiful employee directed me toward the exit immigration tax window.

"I need my 1,400 baht VAT refund to pay my five hundred baht exit tax," I explained.

"The VAT refund office is in the departure lounge," the woman said. "You cannot pass through immigration without paying."

Despite my protests, she shook her head, waved me on, and turned to the next person in line.

An electrical current of panic streaked through my brain. I was stranded in Bangkok, five thousand miles from home, because I couldn't get to the departure lounge. I had no money.

Not one cent.

God, please don't let me miss my plane. It's Christmas. I want to get home to my family. Please, please, Lord, show me what to do.

My neck, shoulder, and back muscles seized into tight knots. Light-headed and weak-kneed, I wobbled to a bank kiosk.

"Can you charge five hundred baht to my credit card and give me cash?"

"We only exchange currency. Why don't you try the ATM over there?"

Panicky sweat rolled down my face. I slipped my credit card into the ATM, but I couldn't figure out how to use the "automatic" teller machine or retrieve my Visa. Through blurry eyes, I spotted the squarish Thai lettering.

Instructions, I suppose. Great. I don't read Thai. I need help and I don't know one person in Bangkok who can help me. And now my Visa card is stuck in this crazy machine!

"How do I get my card out of the ATM?" I howled. My verbal frustration, tears, and "loss of face" drew stares. Five Pakistani bystanders dressed in long, loose-fitting cotton tunics and baggy pants surrounded me. One rescued my card from the machine.

I thanked him and proceeded to the tourist information desk. Little did I know that an infamous Farang beggar, a western Caucasian, routinely held up a sign saying, "I'm four thousand baht short to go back home. Can you help me?"

But my situation was not a ruse.

I poured out my story. "I need five hundred baht for the exit tax. I have a 1,400 baht VAT refund due on the other side of immigration. Can you *please* help me?"

The assistants smiled, shrugged their shoulders, and pointed me back to China Airlines.

The elephant crushing my chest felt as heavy as my overweight carry-ons tugging at my aching arms.

How will I get home? I wish my boss had explained that the VAT refund office was located after exiting immigration.

Tears streamed down my face. I returned to China Airlines to ask for help. The airline employee who took my ticket was checking in another passenger with distinct Thai features—large round eyes, rounded nose, full lips, and sculpted cheekbones.

She seems unusually tall for a Thai—at least six feet tall, maybe taller.

Most Thais stand five foot four.

Distraught, I explained my Catch-22 predicament to the attendant, "If you can just let me go through to the departure lounge, I'll get the money and—"

"Traveling is stressful," the tall Thai woman said in a perfect American accent. "Here, take this."

I stared at the money she thrust into my palm. She had given me one thousand baht, more than enough.

"Thank you. I'll pay you back on the other side of immigration."

"Don't worry about it."

"What's your name?"

"Angela."

I dashed to immigration and slid five hundred baht under the immigration window and was cleared to go into the departure line. Waves of relief and joy refreshed my body as I prayed.

At last, I'm headed home. Wahoo! Thank you, God, for hearing my prayer and providing for me. Now I can get home to celebrate your Son's birth with my two sons.

At the next turnstile, the immigration officer inspected my passport. "You overstayed your visa. That will cost an extra two hundred baht ($54) per day."

She allowed me to collect my refund from the VAT refund office, which paid the remaining overstay fees.

I entered the departure area and looked for Angela.

How did she slip through immigration without my seeing her?

Apprehension drained away, leaving behind hunger pangs. It might be a long time before they served the meals on the plane. After paying at immigration, I still had 250 baht ($8.25)—enough to purchase a sandwich, chips, and my favorite Thai drink, an icy watermelon beverage. While I ate, I looked for Angela. I wanted to get her address so I could mail the money to her.

By the time I finished my food, I still hadn't seen her. I searched every China Airlines waiting lounge—no Angela. I looked carefully. Twice. I even checked the restrooms.

I decided she must already be on the plane, so I boarded my flight home. After takeoff, I walked up and down the two aisles from one end of the plane to the other and looked at every face.

No Angela.

I sat and pondered what had happened that day. I had given freely to those who had no way to repay—just as Jesus taught me to love my neighbor. The tall Thai woman had given just as freely to me, and I couldn't find the stranger to repay her.

Could Angela be an angel? Nah! Couldn't be. But how else can I explain . . . ?

Cold chills rippled up and down my body—and not from the plane's air-conditioning.

Tears of gratitude slid down my cheeks. Unlike Bangkok's street beggars, who depend on the generosity of passersby, or the Farang beggar, who dupes sympathetic givers, I have a generous God who never overlooks my shortages. *Jehovah Jireh*, the God Who Provides for our salvation, gave His Son as an infant at Christmas, and He was still giving and providing.

The One-in-Three-Million Miracle

JAMES STUART BELL

W e've all been in situations where we've just met someone whose home is far away, and we try to find some common ground by telling them we've either visited that place or know someone who lives in the overall vicinity. Sometimes we even discover that there is a loose connection with another person or family, and a bond is established with that newly met person.

My newly met person on a cold winter Christian retreat Sunday in 1976 in Convent Station, New Jersey, turned out, down the road, to be the most significant and cherished individual in my life—my wife. But another person played a role in the background of both of our lives.

When it comes to women, guys are often characterized by their sex drives, not their heads and hearts. But we also have emotional needs to bond, love, protect, and provide. I remember as an adolescent hugging my pillow at night, pretending I was in the arms of my future wife.

The problem was, I had no idea who this person would be, and I wasn't going to let confusing hormones lead me into any snap decisions. I had better things to do like focus on my studies in high school, because if I didn't make the honor roll I wasn't allowed to go to school social events.

As I entered college, I was occupied with trying my hand at rugby and buying beat-up classic cars. I asked big questions about who we are and why we are on this planet, and I dated several girls. Through various Eastern philosophies and mind-expanding drugs, I was led back to the God of my youth and had a life-changing experience with Jesus Christ. But as a twenty-year-old college student, I still had no idea what God wanted me to do with my life.

During my junior year abroad, I lived in a community that housed young men in Dublin, Ireland. My buddy Paddy, an on-fire Christian who set up Bible studies and times of prayer in our home, brought along a girl named Fionnuala one evening. Later, when she heard I was studying Gaelic and writing a paper on Irish storytellers in the original language, she invited me to go with her to the Gaeltacht (Irish-speaking) region on the west coast of County Donegal. We stayed in the whitewashed thatched cottage of a true Irish bard, Neddy Frank a'Grianna, who was the official storyteller in the early '70s. He lived in the village along the windswept rocks, with the surf pounding in the background.

Fionnuala told me that she and her close friend had come to this far-flung village as kids every summer from a little village called Roundwood. Her friend's mother valued the old Irish culture—its music, dancing, language, and oral tradition—and sent the girls packing in order to keep those Irish roots watered and running deep.

One weekend, when Fionnuala had heard about a prayer revival taking place in Dublin, she asked if we guys could gather in the living room and pray. She felt that because of the winds of revival, God would grant us the desires of our hearts.

When it was my turn to speak, she looked penetratingly at me and asked what the desire of my heart was. I thought for a moment and said I didn't have any, but then I realized this might be my big opportunity. So I scrunched up my eyes and suddenly, to my chagrin, blurted out, "I want a wife." Because I was a starving student, I quickly added, "But not right away."

Fionnuala prayed for a moment and confidently said that God would answer that prayer in His time.

As I prayed by my bedside that night, I tried to hem God in a bit and asked Him to give me an Irish wife. I loved the Old World innocence, soft lilting voice, and striking beauty of so many Irish females. The next morning I amended the request, telling God that He knew best and I would accept a wife according to His specifications, not mine.

Fast forward a couple years and I was back in the States, graduated, and ready to look for a job. I went with my parents as they joined my sister at the end of a weekend retreat. It was called a Healing of Relationships weekend and included a Sunday breakfast. We were asked to share testimonies of how God was working. As I was munching on sausage and eggs, from the table behind me I heard the familiar velvety Irish brogue and a young woman saying, "I want to fight and smile and stand up for Christ."

I knew I had to meet this young woman.

As this young lady and I stood in the hall, she told me that she had found a personal relationship with Jesus Christ the night before but had no money left and was returning to Ireland soon because there was nothing for her in the States. I asked her if she had a Bible and if she knew what fellowship with other Christians was all about. Within a couple of weeks I bought her a new Bible, and we were off to our first fellowship meeting together. I was determined to be honorable before God and not exploit the situation of a beautiful and vulnerable young woman looking for guidance.

In the course of the next few church meetings, she told me why she had attended the retreat in the first place. She had met a young American man in Dublin and had come over to marry him but had prayed to God for a sign. Right away she caught the young man in an indiscretion, and she broke the relationship off.

When she heard about the retreat, she thought perhaps a spiritual weekend might heal the rift and that she and her former boyfriend could find God together. He agreed to come and they sat listening to the sermon on the first night. The retreat director spoke about idolatry—not the kind where we worship images, but rather our possessions, our careers, or even our relationships. We can put nothing before God, she learned.

Her ex-boyfriend told her that they should both leave, that this religion was just a crutch for needy people—not them.

She thought for a moment, especially in light of the idolatry sermon, and pointedly asked, "Are you asking me this minute to choose between you and Christ?"

He honestly responded, "Yes, and you have no money and no car to get back."

She boldly proclaimed, "I choose Christ. Good-bye."

Later that night, some women prayed over her and she received Christ. They told her that God would answer her prayer requests. She was a woman who knew what she wanted. She prayed, "Lord, I need a husband and I need him now."

Over the ensuing months we would go to fellowship and later sit in my car and pray together. She knew we were meant to be together, and though I wanted it more than anything, I prayed for a definite sign from God as to whether we should marry.

She soon started to call me "slowcoach," as I continued to deliberate marriage. When God finally conveyed that the decision was mine to make, I was quickly down on one knee by the Cloisters Art Museum on the Hudson River.

I married Margaret Curley three months later, and the deepest desire of my heart was answered, as Fionnuala had prayed two years earlier. God allowed me to find a wife who was Irish, perhaps because of my later retraction in allowing Him to make that call.

I asked Margaret what proved to be a bombshell question the frosty January night we first drove to that fellowship meeting after we met at the retreat. I curiously asked where she was from in Ireland. I thought maybe I could establish the bond I spoke of at the beginning of this story. I had studied in her home country, and perhaps there were some friends of friends of friends. Probably not—Ireland's population at the time was over three million people. So what were the chances?

She told me she came from a small village in County Wicklow named Roundwood; no Americans she knew had heard of it.

"Oh, I've heard of Roundwood. I know someone who lived there."

When I voiced Fionnuala's name, Margaret was dumbfounded—Fionnuala Allen was her friend! As time wore on and we fell in love, God's overarching plan, His intricate design, was more clearly revealed, and we could see how this was a wonderful—and need I say, miraculous—confirmation of our decision.

The girl who took me to the west coast of Ireland and told me about her childhood friend didn't know she was speaking of my future wife. The mother who planned the trips for the two girls was my future mother-in-law. The girl who prophesied that God would answer my desires for a future wife had no idea that she was talking about her own childhood friend.

We tried to find Fionnuala Allen after we were married and returned to Ireland for a visit, but to no avail. To this day we have not located her, but she played an important role in both of our lives at different times. With no previous connections from either Margaret or me, God did a one-in-three-million miracle. Who knows, perhaps God will answer our prayer and we'll cross paths with Fionnuala again in this life, but if not, God willing, we'll meet in heaven.

The Still, Small Voice
of Authority

DELORES CHRISTIAN LIESNER

B arb peeked around the office door she held open, thinking I was right behind her.

"Forget something?" my co-worker asked as I stood there looking perplexed.

Call Ken now; he needs you. The urgent prompting filled my mind and I'd stopped in my tracks, momentarily startled. Thinking of all the errands I had to do, I hesitated.

"What's wrong?" my friend asked.

"I have to call home. Ken needs me," I replied, turning back into the office. She followed as I headed for the nearest desk phone.

"What just happened here?" she asked, looking at me oddly. "Didn't you have a list of errands to do? I didn't hear the phone ring. . . . How do you know he needs you?"

"I just know it's urgent," I said as I dialed our number.

When Ken answered the phone, his voice was weak and my alarm grew.

"Honey, what's wrong?" I asked.

"I don't know," he mumbled. "Sick. Headache. Can't remember if I took aspirin."

My strong hero who never seemed to get ill sounded so far away!

"Do you want me to come home?" I asked, but I was already mentally canceling my errands and trying to calm a mounting fear.

"Yes. I need you."

Barb's eyes widened as I told her something was wrong with Ken and raced toward the parking lot. Her voice echoed, "I'll call you later," as I let the door slam behind me.

My daughter lives next door and happened to be on the porch when I screeched to a halt in front of our house. I yelled for her to get her husband, Frank, in case I needed help.

I found Ken curled up on our bed, mumbling about meatloaf and aspirin. Immediately dialing the triage number of our medical clinic, I thanked God when I was connected with a nurse I knew who calmly instructed me to get Ken to the emergency room and assured me she would set up his initial admittance. Frank helped me get Ken into the car and to the hospital.

By the time we arrived, I knew something was really wrong: Ken could not tell the nurse where he was. A medical team quickly surrounded him with syringes, tubes, and a monitor. When they took Ken for tests, I went back to admittance to sign papers and answer questions. I explained that he had been fine when I left the house in the morning. I also told the admitting nurse about leaving the office to do errands that would take an hour or two when I "heard" the urgent message: *Call Ken now; he needs you.*

Finally, Ken's doctor called to me from behind an emergency room curtain. He explained that Ken had had a stroke and that he had been brought in just in time to receive medication to stop the attack. He questioned me thoroughly about Ken's health and activities that week. Two other doctors joined us, both insisting that Ken must have been ill and called me for help, or that he was ill that morning and I called to check on him, or that we always called each other at that time of day. I felt as if I were being grilled by police. I finally realized the admitting nurse must have repeated my story, and how incredulous it must have sounded.

Each time a doctor suggested what must have "really" happened, I repeated the story for all the onlookers until one doctor raised his eyebrows and asked if I was saying God told me to phone home.

A smile spread across my face as my heart and voice affirmed, "Yes, that is exactly what happened."

The doctor walked away, shaking his head in disbelief, only to return with a neurosurgeon who also wanted to examine Ken and hear the story.

Ken had returned to normal by that time and was amazed to hear what had happened. We were shaken as the doctor explained that if I had done my errands before I returned home, it would have been too late for the medication to help Ken. Sobered, Ken agreed to stay in the hospital overnight for observation. The next day a parade of nurses, doctors, and lab technicians checked on him, shaking their heads in wonder and asking, "Are you the one?"

For several months, repeated testing still showed no damage or other results of a stroke, and I was asked to join Ken for an exit appointment. The goal, the nurse explained, was to see if the patient had omitted telling them about any changes or side effects of the trauma, to see if he indeed had returned to normal. The doctor chuckled when I assured him my husband was as "normal" as I'd ever seen him. And he laughed at Ken's teasing thankfulness that his somewhat rebellious wife had finally listened to a still, small voice of authority.

We all joked, but the lowered tone of the doctor's voice as he left stopped our teasing. The words seemed to hang in the air that the only explanation for Ken's good health was the perfect timing of a "message" to phone home.

The doctor turned the corner and repeated his whispered farewell: "Amazing."

Who's Behind the Wheel?

SHERYL K. JONES

Driving home one day, I spotted a billboard that read, "If Jesus is your copilot, you'd better switch seats." That sign was just another confirmation of God's constant guidance in our lives.

My husband, Randy, and I had been missionaries in Cameroon, Africa. He and his team of national translators had finished translating the New Testament into the Kom language, and our task seemed finished. God directed our steps back to the U.S. and to a little town in Churchill, Montana.

After a few months of our looking for work and finding nothing, I began to wonder if we were in the right place. I not only wondered, I worried. Had God forgotten about us? In October 2006, a local potato farmer approached Randy about working during the harvest season. Randy was grateful to earn a little money.

After the first day on the job, Randy realized that hard work and quick wits were key ingredients to the job. Even his small position required observant eyes. Randy was entrusted with the task of helping unload the trucks swollen with fresh potatoes from the field onto a conveyer belt. He, with others, separated rocks and large dirt clods from the flood of potatoes that poured onto the belt called a "stinger." Then the fresh potatoes were carried to other stations for storing. The rocks and dirt clods were tossed into a large bucket attached to a bulldozer parked directly behind Randy's station.

Every morning Randy was up early and worked all day in cold and rain and heat with the others at the stinger, arriving home after dark, full of dirt and fatigue.

One morning, just after Randy drove away to the farm, I felt compelled to pray. I called the children together.

"Daddy looked awfully tired this morning. We need to pray for him—for strength and for protection. He's working with a lot of dangerous equipment," I explained.

Randy arrived on the scene that brisk October morning as a glowing orange sun appeared on the horizon. A driver backed a full potato truck to the conveyer belt to dump its cargo. Randy and his partner took their places at the stinger, zipped up their jackets, and slid their chilled fingers into worn gloves. They dug into the mountain of spuds the moment they poured off the back of the truck and rumbled and bumped past their stiff fingers.

Some fifteen yards away, another truck of potatoes was in place for the next unloading. The driver parked the truck, turned off the engine, and stepped away to work at another position.

The morning routine progressed as usual. Above the roar of the machinery, Randy talked and joked with his partner while tossing rocks and clods over his shoulder into the bucket of the bulldozer behind him.

Then Randy noticed that his colleague had suddenly stopped responding to him.

Randy glanced up. His co-worker's eyes were growing wider by the moment. His mouth had fallen open, and he stepped backward from the stinger with his eyes fixed on something behind Randy.

Randy turned and froze. The parked truck, still loaded with a ton of potatoes, was rolling down the slope toward the bulldozer directly behind Randy—and it was gaining speed.

In a split second Randy realized there was no escape. When the truck hit the bulldozer, it would pin him between the bucket of rocks in front and the stinger behind, crushing him. No time to think. No time to react.

There was only one possible solution: Someone needed to be in that truck to stop it.

But there was no driver.

Randy watched the unmanned truck race toward him. In those seconds his mind calculated the impact; his body stiffened for the jolt. Then, just before the truck collided into the bulldozer, the truck suddenly veered.

The swerve appeared so abrupt that Randy looked up to see who had suddenly commandeered the truck. The truck missed the bulldozer by inches. Randy watched it roll past and collide into another truck. An echo of metal against metal clanged like a loud cymbal.

A collective gasp hung in the crisp morning air. The truck was driverless.

Every worker stood in place, not moving. What they had witnessed was a miracle and many praised God for Randy's protection. With a slight turning of the wheel at the precise time, God spared Randy's life.

But who turned the wheel? Did the truck turn on its own power?

Or, perhaps, was an angel of mercy in the driver's seat?

When Randy came home that night and told us what had happened, we sat amazed. God had answered our prayer.

The incident reminded me of God's graciousness to teach us necessary lessons. I had been fretting about how God would take care of us, but this runaway-truck episode was a timely lesson of God's providence in our lives.

God's message rang in my mind loud and clear. He was in control. He obviously had a plan for Randy's future in Churchill, Montana. We needed to trust Him to work it out.

A few months later, God's plan became evident. Randy was invited to become the next pastor at Manhattan Bible Church in the town next to ours. I was so glad God was in the driver's seat and steering our future to the exact location He wanted to put us—for His glory and our good.

Door-to-Door Surprise

JANICE RICE

I was doing door-to-door ministry in Fiji, telling people a three-minute Bible story and asking if they wanted prayer. The first house of the day was in a rural farming community where Americans didn't usually visit.

A sweet Hindu woman, Sevita, met us at her rustic gate and invited us in for some tea. We slipped off our flip-flops and stepped into her humble home. It was nicer than most, and she was alone for the day. This was unusual as most families lived together with grandparents and in-laws mixed in.

I sat on her couch with my translator and a team member nearby. I shared the story of the woman with the issue of blood whom Jesus healed after she had been sick for twelve years. Then I asked our hostess if she needed prayer for anything: healing, work, or family issues.

She didn't speak English well and I didn't speak Hindi. She met my eye and held my gaze for a second or two. She told the translator that she had a large hernia on her stomach. She was scheduled to have surgery to remove it in three months. As is common, she didn't have the money for surgery and was afraid. Then she said in Hindi, "Tell her to come with me."

My translator and friend were both male and apparently they weren't invited to come with us.

I followed the woman down a small hallway to her kitchen. She faced me, grabbed my hand, and put it on her stomach. I felt a hernia the size of a grapefruit. Through her thin cotton dress it was visible but not noticeable, since she was a larger woman. As I felt the size of it, I understood the pain this woman must be in. I nodded, removed my hand, and started to pray.

In that split second before praying for healing, doubt inevitably fills your mind. You think to yourself, *Who am I to ask God to heal this woman?*

Then you remind yourself that it's not our power but God's power through us. God looks for available people who are willing to step out in faith. So I began praying by telling God how I was feeling.

"Father," I said, in English, knowing Sevita probably wouldn't understand a word I was saying. "You know I can't do this, but you can. So I ask you to do the impossible. I ask you to eliminate, eradicate, and disintegrate this hernia right now, in Jesus' name. I plead the blood of Jesus over Sevita and ask you to heal her of this hernia completely. Dry it up and remove it from her body."

I paused, not knowing what else to say. God would heal her if He wanted to. I'm not a doctor; I certainly couldn't.

"Amen," I said.

When I looked at Sevita, I was filled with compassion for her. I was strongly convicted that I needed to share the Gospel with her.

"Sevita, God might heal your body, but your spirit needs to be saved," I said with my hand on her shoulder.

She scrunched her eyebrows, not understanding English. We both smiled and giggled, knowing that we couldn't communicate.

"Come with me," I said, heading back into the living room. We sat down and I had my translator say for me, "Sevita, God may heal your body, but when you die someday, it's your spirit that needs to go to heaven with Him."

She nodded in agreement but didn't say anything, so we continued.

"More important than a healthy body is a spirit that knows Jesus as Lord and Savior. Jesus is the Son of God. He lived a sinless life and performed many wonderful miracles. Then, jealous religious men beat Him and nailed Him to a cross, where He died for our sins. But on the third day, Jesus rose from the dead and lives forevermore. He's not just a prophet," I said. "He is God."

Many Hindus will recognize Jesus as just another prophet or god amongst a myriad of gods in their religion. I felt impressed to tell her who Jesus really is.

Sevita held my gaze for what seemed a long time.

"If I ask Jesus to be my Savior . . . will He heal me?" she asked.

Aren't those words worth a million dollars? Who can answer that kind of a question? I thought to myself.

I sat in my chair, sweating. This kind of question didn't deserve a pat answer. She wanted the truth, and she deserved it. My mind was racing and my palms were sweating.

I looked to my translator and fellow team member for help. They both shrugged their shoulders. In my mind, I begged God for help. Then He spoke to me so clearly, I will never forget it. *Faith,* God said. *I honor faith.*

I straightened my shoulders and met Sevita's gaze again.

"Sevita," I began. "God honors faith. It is up to Him whether He heals you or not. I certainly can't do it. But I believe that if you will put your trust in Him, He will honor your faith and heal you. But remember, it's up to Him, not us."

Whew! I think I said all those words in one breath.

She furrowed her eyebrows and continued to gaze at me. Then she slapped her knee with resolution.

"I want to do it," she said in Hindi. "I want to give my life to Jesus."

"Praise God!" I cried. I led her in the sinner's prayer, through the translator. It was incredible. This woman had not felt God heal her yet, but she was putting her trust in Him by faith.

When we finished praying, we stood. Normally, we would say good-bye and head to the next house. But no one was in a hurry to leave. Sevita had the day to herself so she seemed to enjoy the company. She led us back into her kitchen for some juice and cookies. She pointed out her baby chickens in a box to one side of her kitchen. So we played with the baby chicks for a few minutes. We admired the sugarcane fields her husband and sons worked so hard in. She showed us family pictures. Then we hugged her and stepped outside to continue to her neighbors' homes.

I glanced over my shoulder to see her standing under her covered porch, watching us leave. Her face was different. She smiled and waved her hand in farewell. What a wonderful morning it had been, and it was only 9:30!

The next day, after more door-to-door ministry in a different neighborhood, our team gathered at a local pizza restaurant. We had invited the youth of our host church and their pastor to join us. As we laughed, ate pizza, and chugged soda—just as we do with youth group kids in the United States—their pastor walked in. He sat next to me.

"Oh, Pastor," I said, suddenly remembering Sevita. "We gave your business card to a woman out in Ba named Sevita. She gave her life to the Lord yesterday. Your local pastor will need to follow up with her."

"Yes," the pastor answered. "She already called me."

"We prayed for her yesterday," I continued, not really hearing him. "She accepted Jesus . . . Wait! She called you already?"

"Yes," the pastor said with a smile. "She wanted me to tell you that she is healed."

"She is healed?" My heart raced with amazement.

"The hernia is completely gone."

I started laughing and clapping my hands. "She got healed!" I called to the young man who had translated for me the day before. "She got healed!" I told my team member. "Sevita is completely healed."

Everyone cheered.

I sat in awe as I finished my pizza and soda. My mind was trying to wrap around the details of the incomprehensible. This is how miracles are—supernatural highlights in our mundane lives. God performs them to show average people His incredible love for them. But one of the side benefits is that those He uses to pray feel just as blessed as those He heals!

Faith, God whispered. *I honor faith.*

Angel in the Mirror

SALLY EDWARDS DANLEY

Grammy, when Daddy's not home, his new wife, Estelle, is mean to Melissa. She slaps her face and spanks her. We don't know why. But we don't want her to be our mama anymore."

The voice of the four-year-old made me want to cry. "Grammy" was my best friend, Josie, and I'd gone to Josie's house to help with her three granddaughters for the weekend while her husband, Tom, was working out of town on a construction job.

I'd heard so much about Josie's granddaughters that I had looked forward to helping.

The girls' dad, Peter, was the younger of Josie and Tom's two sons. He and his new wife, Estelle, were on a weekend getaway.

It was about an hour after Peter left when little Teena suddenly told of her new stepmother's cruelty.

"Yeah, Grammy," piped up Barby, the youngest, who was three. "An' she spanks 'lissa. I don't like to see my sissy cry." Her tears surfaced as she spoke.

Josie and I were both shocked.

Melissa, five, was walking slowly across the room toward Josie with her head hung low. She remained silent as her sisters spoke. Then she looked up at Grammy, who opened her arms. Melissa crawled onto Josie's lap. Then the other two joined her. I was sitting beside them on the couch. When Barby climbed into my lap, I was delighted in how easily she trusted me.

Josie and I gathered the three little ones around us like mother hens.

Melissa had tried not to cry when her sisters reported the abuse. But feeling safe at last, she sobbed in her grandmother's arms. All three sobbed. Josie and I even had tears trickling down our cheeks.

A week earlier, during our routine Saturday breakfast at a local restaurant, Josie had told me that Estelle seemed to be having difficulty adjusting to the girls. She had never had children nor been married. Being a mother to three young, energetic stepdaughters was not easy.

Now, after hearing that report from both girls, Josie was shaken. But she didn't know what to do. A very gentle woman, she was too timid to tell anyone—even Tom.

I was grateful that I was there so she didn't have to carry that emotional load alone.

Josie and I agreed that Tom would be enraged if he knew what their granddaughters had said. When he was younger he'd had a violent temper. Church involvement had settled him down. Still, Josie and I agreed he didn't need to know yet. She kept the girls' stories to herself until she could verify them.

For the next couple of weeks, more reports spilled out from the younger girls about several other incidents. We determined that Estelle would hit Melissa instead of one of the younger ones who had actually done wrong. None of the girls told their dad. Melissa just accepted the punishment silently.

Josie and I were frustrated because we didn't know how to stop it. I suggested she tell Peter or the authorities. But she didn't want to upset Peter or Tom. She was afraid of them turning against her, especially since she didn't have proof.

Feeling powerless, one Saturday I suggested we pray and ask God to protect the girls. Josie quickly agreed. She grabbed my hand across the table and asked me to pray.

I said, "Lord, Josie and I know you are especially protective of helpless little children. We know you can keep them from harm. So, Lord, we ask you to send a mighty angel to guard and protect little Melissa from Estelle. Thank you, Lord, for stationing that angel in her bedroom."

A week later, Josie and I took Melissa shopping for school clothes. We had left Teena and Barby at home with Tom.

Melissa was so happy to be treated like a big girl. We chatted about the importance of her starting kindergarten the next month. We were three girls out shopping and having fun talking.

The sun was setting when we left the shopping center. As we walked across the huge parking lot toward Josie's car, Melissa stared at the brilliant pole lights.

Suddenly, she said, "That's almost as bright as my angel in the mirror."

Josie and I stopped abruptly. We were shocked with her unexpected comment.

"Oh, do you have an angel lamp, Melissa?" I asked.

"No," she said. "It's a real angel in my big mirror. When I went to bed I used to be really scared. But now at night this beautiful glowing angel is always in the mirror on my dresser. She's so big she fills up the whole mirror. She sings real soft to me and I know she'll keep me safe. She makes it easy to go to sleep."

Josie looked relieved and whispered that she hadn't heard anything from the other girls lately about Melissa being struck.

We drove back to Josie's house, listening to Melissa jabbering happily.

The next week Peter and Estelle separated. Later he told Josie what had happened. One evening he had gone to say good-night to Melissa in her bedroom. When he opened the door, he saw Estelle shaking the child and scolding her in a whisper. He was furious and ordered Estelle out of the room. He soothed his crying child and held her until she relaxed and was ready to sleep.

Peter was furious and wasn't sure what to do. Finally, he realized he couldn't trust his girls alone with Estelle anymore. So he asked her to leave that night. His daughters were more important to him than a cruel woman, and eventually the marriage ended.

The girls never said anything else about what had happened after we prayed. We only know Melissa was definitely guarded by an angel. We suspect it had in some way brought Peter into the room at the right time. Regardless, we were thankful for that angel in the mirror.

Gracious Intervention

WALTER B. HUCKABY

I arrived in Vietnam in late January of 1968. I remember the excitement of the sailor who moved the stairway to our plane so that we could get off. He told us that rockets had hit the base the night before. He pointed down the runway to a hangar with a huge hole in the roof from the attack.

This was the day after the infamous Tet Offensive began. The North Vietnamese had launched attacks all over South Vietnam, taking our forces by surprise. I heard machine gun fire in the distance. I realized that I was in a war zone.

I was uneasy being away from my wife, Kezia, and daughter, especially since we thought our next child was on the way. My deployment was to be just over a month, so I would be back in time for the birth of our second.

The time passed fairly quickly in Vietnam. I met some other Christians frequently for prayer and Bible study. My job each day was to supervise the electronics repair shop for our two squadron airplanes, another man's job was telephone repair and installation, and the third man's job was to bomb North Vietnam. Our daily Bible study and prayer strengthened me for some tough times ahead.

After I returned to my family on the island of Guam, we settled into the routine of waiting for the next child. I worked as an aviation electronics technician for the U.S. Navy. Things were going well until one Sunday morning when we were getting ready for church. Kezia suddenly began to bleed profusely. I rushed her to the hospital.

What appeared to be a normal pregnancy was actually a molar pregnancy that developed into a deadly, fast-growing cancer: choriocarcinoma. Doctors operated to stop the bleeding and to find a blood vessel that had not collapsed so they could give Kezia a transfusion to replace the loss of over half of her blood supply. They were able to save her life. They kept her in the hospital for testing to determine what had caused the bleeding.

On Thursday I was called back to the hospital to hear the diagnosis. It was cancer. The tumor had broken open a blood vessel. The cancer, originating in the uterus, had spread through the lymphatic system to the lungs. The X rays showed that the cancer was growing in the lungs and was being spread throughout her body via the bloodstream.

This cancer, if caught early, is usually treatable. But in this case, the rapidly growing cancer was very far along.

I remember driving away from the hospital to pick up my toddler daughter. I wept as I realized my little girl might grow up without a mother. I had lost my mother at age seven and remembered very little about her. My preschool daughter would probably have no memory of her mother.

I also remember that in the midst of the overwhelming sorrow, I had a deep sense of peace and trust in the Lord.

Philippians 4:6–7 reflects the peace that the Lord gave me in this situation:

> Don't worry about anything; instead, pray about everything. Tell God what you need, and thank him for all he has done. Then you will experience God's peace, which exceeds anything we can understand. His peace will guard your hearts and minds as you live in Christ Jesus.

I had been a follower of Jesus for five years and had learned to trust the Lord in all circumstances. This was easily the most intense test so far! How was it possible to face the probable death of my wife, with all of the accompanying sorrow, and yet have a deep inner peace? As the Scripture says, this peace transcends all understanding.

I made several long-distance phone calls. One was to my father, who worked as a psychiatric technician at Porterville State Hospital in California. He checked with the doctors at the hospital. They told him that the cancer at this point was terminal.

I also called some friends in a church we had attended and where we first met, fell in love, and were married. They were getting ready to attend a Bible conference in Yosemite

National Park. We told them Kezia's condition, and they promised to ask those at the conference to pray; hundreds of believers from churches all over the West Coast prayed for her. Many of them took this request home with them and expanded the prayer support with perhaps thousands of others.

The navy moved quickly, putting my wife on an airplane to transfer her to the naval hospital in Oakland, California. The airplane was filled with casualties from the Vietnam War, including the mayor of Saigon. The plane took Kezia to Travis Air Force Base in California, where she was put in an ambulance to be taken to the Oak Knoll Naval Hospital.

At the hospital, my wife overheard a doctor tell another doctor that Kezia was in for a hysterectomy. She objected. She didn't want them to do anything until I got there. She was committed to having more children.

Meanwhile, I was still in Hawaii. The navy had given me emergency leave so that I could travel to see my wife in California. It was easy to get from Guam to Hawaii with my toddler; however, the flights from Hawaii to California were fully booked. Since I was on emergency leave, I could bump a passenger and get on the plane, but my daughter could only get on a plane with an empty seat. It took us twenty-four hours before we arrived in Southern California.

Finally, I got to see my wife in the hospital. When she saw the look on my face, she reassured me that everything would be okay. The assurance did not come from the doctors. It came from the Lord through the Scriptures.

She had read these verses: "He has saved me from death, my eyes from tears, my feet from stumbling. And so I walk in the Lord's presence, as I live here on earth!" (Psalm 116:8–9).

She could not believe it. Was this really the Lord telling her that she was going to survive this dreadful disease? She continued to read and found these verses: "I will not die; instead, I will live to tell what the Lord has done. The Lord has punished me severely, but he did not let me die" (Psalm 118:17–18).

Kezia believed that the Lord was giving her His assurance of survival. She comforted me with this. Although I did not have the same sense of assurance, I was encouraged at her positive feelings.

They continued the chemotherapy for two months.

I received new orders transferring me to the local naval base, Alameda Naval Air Station. I checked in and went to work as the shop supervisor for the radar and communication/navigation shops.

After a while, the chemotherapy began to have some mild side effects. My wife's throat became sore, but the Lord spared her from what normally would have been severely painful side effects.

After about two months, Kezia was discharged from the hospital with the cancer gone. They said that if it did not come back in five years, it would be considered a complete cure. It has been over forty-five years; it is a complete cure!

The doctor who treated Kezia on Guam came through the area a few years later, following up on some of his cases. He was stunned to hear that she had survived. And she not only survived cancer of the uterus, but she also gave birth to three more children. We are thankful for the skill and expertise of the U.S. Navy in treating cancer. We are even more thankful for what we believe was the intervention of the Lord in answer to the prayers of His people. The advanced state of this very rapidly growing cancer should have resulted in Kezia's death.

I thank the Lord for His gracious intervention!

When I hear of people afflicted with terminal cancer, I continue to pray for them. Perhaps the Lord will intervene in their lives, as well.

Angels Are Watching Over Me

ALICE M. MCGHEE

Everything went black, but it wasn't "black." All I could see were swirls of pink and blue.

The colors moved as if someone were making cotton candy with pink- and blue-colored sugar spinning in the machine. I heard only silence—but it was deafening. I felt as if I were going to die.

"If you are ready for me, I am ready for you," I told Jesus in my heart.

Everything stopped. As I sat in my car, I knew the engine had stalled, but it felt like my body was still spinning. The top of my head hurt horribly. As my jumbled mind tried to figure out where I was, I tried to open the driver's side door of the car, but it would not open.

The car had landed in the midst of a grove of saplings. The driver's side door was pushed against them so tightly it could not open. I became vaguely aware of cars and trucks moving along on the highway above me, way above me. I wasn't sure where I was. I wondered if I had died and gone to heaven.

There was a knock on the front passenger-side door. An average-looking man with sandy hair and glasses, who was wearing a red shirt, said, "Lady, are you all right?"

He was not wearing a coat even though it was snowing hard and the ground was icy. I was not sure where he had come from or how he had gotten there.

"I think I'm okay, but I'm not sure."

"We need to get you out of this car. It's leaking gas. Can you crawl to the passenger side door in the backseat?"

"I think I can."

"Move back that way and I'll try to help you. No, wait! Your car is at a precarious angle. Come out the front passenger door. I'm afraid the car might tip over if you try to get out by any other way. Move very carefully!"

As I slid across the seat toward the sound of his voice, I was not afraid. I trusted him completely, even though we had never met.

Mr. Red Shirt said, "Let's move away from the car. You have a gas leak. The odor is pretty strong."

I gradually became more aware of my surroundings. I did smell the pungent odor from the leaking gas. There was a steep slope a short distance away from my car, and I realized that the hill was covered with snow and ice.

The snow had been falling for quite a while. I wondered how I would be able to climb up to the road. Snow and ice had made the road slippery and started my predicament. I walked toward the slope that led to the road, but it was difficult due to the slick and uneven ground.

My new friend told me to take his arm and he would help me climb the hill. As I placed my arm through his, the grass was no longer slippery. Walking up the hill became easy, even though the ground was still covered with ice and snow.

I heard a siren and saw the flashing lights of a fire truck. As my friend and I reached the interstate highway at the top of the hill, I was placed into the caring hands of the firefighters.

One of the firefighters asked where my car was.

"It's down at the bottom by some trees."

He went down into the ravine to be sure no one else had been in the car with me. It took him quite a while to find the car because the snow and darkness hindered the visibility.

The EMT taped my head and neck in a restraint because I told him most of my spine had been previously fused. They handled me gently.

The firefighter who had been searching for my car returned to the ambulance and said, "Most people who park their cars that far from the highway don't walk away from them! No one else is in your car. I think you should keep driving big, heavy cars like that Park Avenue. The size of that car is probably one reason you're alive."

"Where is the man in the red shirt who got me out of the car and helped me up the hill? I want to thank him for his help."

"He was standing right here next to the ambulance just a minute ago," one of the men said. "Hey, John, have you seen the guy wearing the red shirt who saw the accident? I was looking for him so I could ask him a few questions. It was like he just disappeared. He was here and then he wasn't. I didn't even see his car. I have no idea how he got out here. It is the weirdest thing I have ever seen."

The ambulance ride to the hospital was uneventful. After a CAT scan, the doctors decided I was in remarkably good condition and could go home. Officer Johnson came into the exam room where I waited with my husband. He asked where I had been and where I was going. I told him I had been at choir practice at my church and was getting ready to make the turn off the highway to go the rest of the way home. The officer said I wasn't near the turnoff.

"You don't really know where you were, do you?" Officer Johnson asked. He said that the tow truck driver had used 150 feet of cable to pull the car out of the ravine. He was incredulous. He had tried to trace my tire tracks. So many cars had problems with the icy roads that the tracks were a jumble. He decided that he couldn't give me a ticket because he wasn't sure what I had done other than probably drive too fast for road conditions. He cautioned me to drive carefully in the future and said I could go home.

With my head still pounding, my husband and I drove to the repair shop where my car had been towed. At first it didn't look too bad, but the mechanic told us the frame of the car had been twisted, the motor had been knocked off the mounting, and the gas tank was ruptured.

The strangest thing was that each of the foot compartments had been shoved upward nearly to the bottom of the seats, except for one—the one in front of the driver's seat.

"I like your bumper sticker," the mechanic said, "the one that says 'Angels are watching over me.' I know somebody was watching over you, or you would not have walked away from that banged-up car the way you did. Do you believe in God?"

"I most certainly do! God is my life and my salvation." I then walked over to where the car was parked and gently rubbed my hand over the bumper sticker and said a quiet prayer. "God, thank you for sending your angels to watch over me. I recognize the power of your protection. Without you I would have died."

My husband, Ken, went to the crash location to see what he could figure out. From looking at the tire marks, he said I must have gone down into the ravine with the back end of the car first. This pushed my spine into the back of the driver's seat, providing support—something I desperately needed since I'd been through several surgeries and my spine had been fused. Had the front of the car gone down first, I can only imagine what kind of shape my back would have been in!

As I thought back to the bumper sticker, I knew I had a lot to be thankful for. I don't know why God decided to spare my life, but He obviously wasn't finished with me.

As I had driven to church that night for choir practice, I didn't know how badly I would need God before the night was over. After all, it was only a short distance. I was all set to make the drive based on my own skill and strength.

I learned to trust God with *everything* on that night. Trusting myself was not enough. Not only did God watch over me when I had not asked Him to, but He had a whole army of angels there—including one wearing a red shirt!

The Key to God's Power

BOB HASLAM

A revival spirit characterized the meetings in the Michigan church I pastored. This was the first church I'd served after seminary, and services were different back then than they are in today's contemporary format.

Each Sunday morning I gave an evangelistic message and invited people to accept Christ as their Savior. Over a few weeks, several seekers accepted Christ and became active in our church. Many people were praying for others to come to faith in Christ and invited their friends to church. Our attendance grew, and members came to church expecting to see people of all ages make decisions to accept Christ.

We provided discipleship classes for the new believers, and the congregation was electric with anticipation of even more people coming to the Lord. New Christians told their friends about their newfound trust in Christ, and spiritual momentum climbed. Even young people were witnessing at school.

A young couple faithfully attended our Sunday morning services. When we sang a song of invitation, tears flowed down their faces. Yet they made no move to come forward. I was concerned, knowing they might stop coming to church to avoid the conviction they felt when they heard God's Word preached. I sensed how important it was for them to make a decision for Christ before they began to pull away from God's tug on their hearts. The Lord impressed me with the need to fast and pray for this couple and others who were attending services but had not made their peace with God.

One icy Michigan evening, the Lord prompted me to drive to the young couple's home and invite them to open their hearts to the Lord. I went to the garage, started my car, and began to back out into the driveway. Quickly I realized the car had a flat tire. I had changed tires before and planned to quickly take care of the problem and go on my mission.

I placed the trunk key into the lock and turned it. To my horror, the key broke off. I knew I was in trouble. Wistfully, I placed the stub of the key into the lock and tried repeatedly to open the trunk lid. Of course, it didn't work. My wife was not home, and there was no close neighbor I could call upon to help me, so I called upon the Lord.

"Lord, I pray that when I place the key into the lock, it will open the lid," I implored. As sure as I was that the Lord had prompted me to venture forth that evening, I dared to ask for the impossible. I remembered the Scripture verse, "And we are confident that he hears us whenever we ask for anything that pleases him" (1 John 5:14). I felt I was in God's will going on this mission, and thus was asking according to His will for Him to enable me to go.

Almost with misgiving, I placed the key stub into the lock and attempted to turn it. To my utter joy, the mangled key turned the lock and opened the trunk lid. I took out the spare tire and jack, lifted the car, changed the tire, and soon was ready to head out. I placed the flat tire and jack into the trunk and shut the lid.

As I drove to the young couple's home, I had a sense of divine intervention and approval of this mission. I no longer hoped the couple would be home. I knew they would be there and that God was in total control. Anticipation gripped my heart as I drove the country road. I was never more convinced that God was leading me.

I arrived, went to their front door, and rang the doorbell. They warmly welcomed me into their home, and we sat down to chat for a while. Then I told them the purpose of my visit. I told them the Lord had impressed upon my spirit that I should visit them and invite them to accept the Lord as their Savior.

"I'm so glad you have come tonight," the wife said as her tears began to flow. "All week I've wished we had gone forward last Sunday."

I opened my Bible and they were ready. That evening, salvation came to that home.

The next morning, I struggled repeatedly to open my car's trunk, but all my efforts were in vain. I realized God had intervened the night before in a special way, and I would have to have professional help to repair my car lock. I drove to a locksmith who had worked for me before. When I told him my story, he seemed incredulous.

"Pastor Haslam, are you sure of what you are telling me? There is no way you should have been able to open the trunk lid with a broken key."

"Do you believe in miracles?" I asked.

"Not really," he replied. "I've seen broken keys many times, and never have I seen a lock turn using one of them."

The locksmith used an instrument to remove the broken piece of key from the lock and made a new key. "Make several keys for me," I instructed with a laugh.

"I still find it hard to believe your story, Pastor Haslam. But if it's true, I agree that this would be a miracle."

To this day, I treasure the memory of God's divine intervention, making that visit possible for me that evening. I actually saw two miracles that night. Not only did the mangled key work, but also the mangled hearts of the young couple were ready, which was also part of God's miracle of grace.

God Protects the Weak

MARLENE ANDERSON

We believe your son has cerebral palsy of the worst magnitude. We are not even sure how much he is able to think or process information. You will need to get a brace made as soon as possible, although we are not sure he can learn to walk."

I sat there, unable to breathe or move. My world stopped when the words of the young intern echoed in my ear.

He spoke in a detached manner as if he were talking about some remote clinical case rather than the ten-month-old baby I held. He hadn't waited until my husband could join us, nor had he prepared me for the earth-shattering news he'd just delivered.

"Do you have any questions?" he asked calmly. When I shook my head, he added, "We'll have a more conclusive diagnosis in a few days, when all the tests are done."

As he left the room, I hugged my baby tightly and struggled with the enormity of what I had just heard. Just the day before, we'd arrived at this medical school hospital. My son was here for observation and evaluation because he couldn't hold up his head.

On the way home, my husband and I talked about the different ways we could still do things together as a family. With a seven-year-old son and six-year-old daughter, we were committed to making life as normal as possible. But when we arrived home, once again the enormity of the challenge we faced struck with full force. I fell to my knees. "Lord, I know this is a reality that I have to face. But God, we need your strength to help us raise our son. Help us make his life as normal as possible, and give him every opportunity to grow up independent and live a good life."

The peace that followed not only filled my heart and being, but also flooded the room. As I got up, I was comforted, encouraged, and motivated.

The following day a doctor we had seen six months before the hospital evaluation, whose early diagnosis had been that Don was born with severe loss of muscle tissue and weakness in the neck, was now saying that they really did not know what was wrong with my son. I was overwhelmed.

But we experienced God's intervention later that week when I took Don back to see this discerning physician. After examining Don, he exclaimed, "If this child has cerebral palsy, then I don't know my business. I see more than 365 cerebral palsy patients a year, and I teach the subject at the medical school."

It seemed his earlier diagnosis of weak or absent muscle tissue was accurate. I left, knowing beyond a shadow of doubt that God would be with my child as he grew up.

My son received a special brace that held up his head. A felt band around his forehead connected to a molded head-piece that was attached with a swivel to a metal rod that went down his back. Straps from that metal rod buckled around his stomach and hips, anchoring it all in place. This enabled Don to stand upright and hold his head securely so he could learn to walk.

But learning to walk was full of risk, even though we knew we had to let him be as independent as possible. Whenever he fell, his head would pop out of the protective felt band and strike the floor first. I was taught to look for signs of concussion. While he did get some goose eggs, he never had a concussion or cut on his head. He quickly learned how to balance and was soon toddling around.

During this time period, we were building a home that would meet the needs of our expanding family. We did a lot of the work ourselves and moved in before the house was completed. One unfinished project was carpet installation.

I was vacuuming the bare floors when my two older children came home from school. My son was in first grade and my daughter was in kindergarten. Don was still learning the joy of early toddling, and he loved to circle from the living room to the dining room to the hallway and back to the living room.

The door leading to the unfinished basement was in the hallway. I reminded my older children several times not to go down to the basement or open the basement door. As they ran upstairs to their bedrooms to play, I made a last check to be sure the door was securely closed before resuming vacuuming.

I was totally engrossed in my job when a voice as loud as if someone were standing beside me said, "It's okay; your son is safe."

Startled and shaking, I shut off the vacuum cleaner. I realized that I had not seen Don come back around that circle.

As fear rose, I hurried to the hallway. The basement door was open. With my heart pounding, I looked down the uncompleted wooden steps. My son was sprawled on the concrete landing below.

I raced down the steps and picked him up. He was crying lightly. His head was still held securely in his brace. He had a small bump on his forehead, but no bruises or broken bones.

I realized I had just experienced a miracle, because the only way Don could have landed at the bottom of those stairs was by falling headfirst. After a few minutes he stopped crying and wanted to continue walking.

We had no idea how the door got open. I had checked it. My children were upstairs playing and had not come down. And we believed Don was too little to have opened it. Was God trying to tell me that no matter how careful I was, I wouldn't be able to protect my son as only He could and would?

As I whispered my prayers of humble thanksgiving, I knew God had sent an angel to warn me about the fall, just as He had sent an angel to protect my son's fall. Although I didn't see the angel, I heard his voice. I also knew that God would protect my son throughout his lifetime, and that I could rest in that assurance during any scary moments that lay ahead.

The Half-Mile Celestial Bowl

JOHN C. MANNONE

It was just another ordinary November afternoon. We prayed for safety; then I kissed my wife good-bye, climbed into my single-engine airplane, and prepared to take off from McMinn County Airport in rural eastern Tennessee—bound to where I worked in southwest Michigan.

I had made many such trips before.

After I copied my instrument flight clearance on the phone, I had fifteen minutes to start the engine, taxi the plane, and finish my preflight procedures before becoming airborne.

The engine sounded good as the Archer II accelerated down the runway and rotated to climb. My wings slipped through a wet canopy of stratocumulus clouds. The mist muted aqua-colored silos, while earth-brown hills turned flat gray.

The engine guzzled avgas to quench its thirst, and the hooves of 180 horses pounded a smooth rhythm like mustangs running wild, moisture glistening on their manes. But there was no sunset to marvel at—only the inside of whitewashed clouds and the white needles on black instruments on my panel. I watched those gauges and dials closely. They were my Braille in blinding clouds.

Air traffic controllers in darkened rooms below also helped me see. With every sweep of their radar eyes, my reflection on their screens was painted electric green. They reassured me that my flight path was clear above the tall pines growing on the Kentucky hills.

The chilly air wafted inside my cabin vents. It was nine degrees colder than forecast at six thousand feet, but 44 degrees was still well above freezing.

I've flown for more than a thousand hours, and I've learned not to tempt the laws of nature—the laws of God. I'd heard it a hundred times before: There are old pilots and there are bold pilots, but there aren't many old, bold pilots.

My plane was not certified to fly in icing conditions—the extra weight and loss of lift could degrade my performance by 40 percent. So I made a precautionary call on the radio to flight service. They reassured me that there was no ice forecast anywhere on my flight route, and that the closest was a hundred miles north of my destination, Benton Harbor, Michigan.

But the air, heavy with moisture, whispered a different story. Drops began to pelt the wings and dance on the Plexiglas windshield. The air continued to hold a chilling portent.

Huntingburg, Indiana, my fuel stop, was blanketed in clouds five hundred feet above the ground. Visibility was at "minimums," and I had to make a missed approach before the runway lights pierced through the atmospheric lace of clouds, allowing me safe visual guidance to the runway.

The sleek white plane with red and blue stripes rested on the tarmac while I studied the weather for any new developments. I'd have a seventy-mile swath of rain to go through.

With clouds layered to thirty thousand feet and the rainy front extending hundreds of miles to the east and west, there was no way of escaping it. I just had to be extra careful about carburetor icing—I didn't want the fuel feeding my engine to be choked off because of moisture freezing in the air-fuel mixing chamber.

I took the necessary precautions and heated the intake air at the cost of performance.

I cruised at four thousand feet. The engine was doing well. Its thrum through the moderate rain was almost soothing. But the air temperature was much cooler now, 38 degrees and dropping. The weatherman offered no wisdom, no explanation.

At 34 degrees, I asked Indianapolis Approach for a lower altitude. They allowed me to descend to three thousand feet—no lower—but the temperature kept dropping.

Thirty-three degrees . . .

Thirty-two degrees, as the water drops continued chilling.

I didn't need a master's degree in physical chemistry to know that water freezes at 32 degrees. Frost began to form on the wings; my windshield glazed over. I could almost hear the ice's mocking cry as it wound frosted fingers around the vital metal parts of my plane, coating all my vulnerable airfoils. Those frozen fingers might as well have been around my throat.

That ice would soon spoil the smooth, lift-sustaining air over the wings. My wings would tire in ice-cold hopelessness.

The ceilings had seriously degraded all around, and I agreed with Indianapolis Approach that I should retreat for warmer air. But there was no warmer air. An unforecasted icy layer had wedged in the entire area. Taking the risk of collecting more ice in a climb—to likely cooler air—would have been tragic.

On my lap lay open the approach plates into Putnam County Airport in Greencastle, Indiana. My electronics told me I was right over it. If only my space-borne allies—those robot birds with radio eyes—could guide me to this fair haven beneath the sleet.

I suppressed the fleeting urge to blindly spiral down through the murk of clouds. There was no wisdom in that, only foolishness. Instead, I declared an emergency instrument approach into the airport, following the proper procedures.

Indianapolis vectored me to the approach course. My gyroscopes spun and seemed to shout for discipline. I finally intercepted the VOR (very high frequency omnidirectional range), a special kind of electronic beacon, whose electronic spoke I could follow to the airport. I was nineteen miles out. And I was picking up more ice.

Established on the final approach course, I cranked my flaps down. They creaked like frosted feathers. I strained to see through washed-out white, but there was no hint of refuge. I was still in the clouds, and I could descend no further. Soon, tall towers would rise in my path—and unforgiving hills with hard-limbed oaks.

My distance-measuring equipment panel glared red. Its lights taunted me as it counted down every tenth of a mile to the missed approach point, where either I would safely descend to land if I could see the airfield or climb out to meet another vagary. I hurled there at almost two hundred feet per second.

I didn't want to dwell on the fact that this might be my last flight, but my knuckles were turning white gripping the control wheel. A flash of my wife's face encouraged me to try harder.

Things were happening too fast for prayer, but I prayed anyway, in between heartbeats. Only a furtive glimpse of the ground occasionally teased me.

As the dial ticked off the last tenth of a mile, my hand moved to the throttle and began to shove it forward to climb. A futile climb, I knew, in my icy coffin; my tears had already frozen in their tracks. Yet in that last instant, in that final second, my prayer must have lifted the fog just high enough above my fuselage to show the concrete runway right below, but only for a moment.

As I swooped to land, those clouds raced furiously to hide my tomorrow. There was nothing but gray all around me. But I had been redeemed. My wheels touched ground and rolled to a quiet stop. And I could finish my prayer.

I remained in the parked plane for many minutes, in sweat and in prayer, before I disembarked. I learned from the airport manager—the field base operator—that Indianapolis Approach had called Putnam County Airport to alert them to my situation and asked them to have emergency vehicles on standby. They didn't think I would make it.

When the manager heard me making my position calls on the radio, he observed a rapidly moving three-hundred-foot layer of clouds about to envelop the airport. The minimums for this approach were around 550 feet.

"He's not going to make it!" he had said.

But my God preserved me, and He waited until the last instant to make His point—trust in Him.

And I did.

Days later, when my mind was clear, I analyzed the details of the weather. Amazingly, the Holy Spirit had allowed me to make complex calculations in my head. And even though I have advanced degrees in chemistry and physics, those calculations require impressive computers.

There is no doubt in my mind that He miraculously allowed a half-mile-wide bowl to appear solely above the airport at the instant of my arrival, barely long enough for me to descend to safety, which was contrary to existing and developing weather conditions.

He was saying to me, "Know that I am God." I had been a Christian for only a year at that time, and it did indeed buttress my faith.

Don't Trust Bow, Sword, or Metal Door

SHERYL K. JONES

rack!
In an instant, I was wide awake.

I heard our dogs' frenzied barking coming from the backyard.

"What is it?" I asked my husband, jarred from a deep sleep. I checked my alarm clock; it was after eleven o'clock in our little village of Belo, Cameroon.

Randy was already dressed. "Not sure. Gonna check."

I sat up in bed while Randy flicked on a flashlight. A steady beam cut through the gloom as he walked toward the living room. The night was warm, but I began to shiver.

"Electricity's out." Randy's voice echoed down the long hallway.

"Did you check the door? Is it locked?" I jumped out of bed and grabbed my robe. I tried to keep my voice down so I wouldn't wake the children. My heart pounded and my hands shook as I fumbled to tie the sash around my robe.

It was January, after the New Year festivities. It was also dry season. Since we'd been missionaries in this location for a few years, we knew what that combination of events meant—the perfect time for thieves to attack. They could travel by dry roads, wreak havoc, and flee without being caught.

My mind was fixed on our metal front door being properly secured.

Is the bolt securely pushed into place in the cement floor? I wondered. Our windows were barred, but the front door needed the large bolt in place.

"It's secure," Randy called back. "But our security light is out. Everything's out."

"Are you sure the bolt's down?" I anxiously insisted.

"Yeah, I . . ."

"Don't shoot," mumbled a voice from outside.

Randy raced back to our bedroom.

"Quick," he said, panting. "It's thieves. They could have guns."

Icy fear grabbed me.

"Get dressed. Quick," Randy instructed. "Go to the kids' room and lock the door behind you until I tell you what to do."

I pulled a T-shirt over my head and dashed to the kids' room, locking the door behind me.

Forgot a flashlight! I cursed myself. I sat quietly on the edge of the girls' bed.

Randy began yelling out every window. Room to room he went, yelling for help in English and then in the language spoken by the people. Our dogs continued to yelp from behind the fence. They managed to keep the intruders in the front yard, where the metal door fortified our position.

As Randy kept calling for help, my hope waned. Minutes seemed to pass like hours with no response from our neighbors.

Then I heard the back door open. My heart stopped beating. The dogs' warning cries stopped. I gripped the edge of the bed and held my breath.

I heard the screen door and then the back door squeak open again. A moment later I heard clicking sounds against the cement floor. Randy must have let one of the dogs in, I realized as I heard him quietly whisper instructions. He had a good idea. Cameroonians feared dogs, so a dog inside might keep the attackers at bay.

I waited for a warning bark to erupt, but the house remained silent. Outside, the other dog started barking again. Randy encouraged the dog inside to do the same.

"Come on, Igelina, give a bark. You can . . . oh no!"

I jumped to my feet. "What happened?"

"I just stepped in a puddle."

"A puddle?"

"Yeah, from the dog."

"Oh no," I replied. Fortunately, the children were still asleep.

"Igelina won't bark." Randy sounded disappointed. "I'm letting her out."

"Be careful," I warned.

I heard the door creaking open, the clambering of claws, and a sudden eruption of barking outside from both dogs. Then the door clicked shut.

I leaned my body against the children's door and felt like a tire that just had all its air let out. A chill crept into the room, but I fought the panic rising in me. Like my husband, I resolved to hope that help was on the way.

Courtney, our nine-year-old, stirred. For the children's sake, I determined to be strong. On wobbly knees, I found my way back to the bed and waited.

Randy came to the door.

"No one's responding. I heard several voices out there."

"They want money," I said, trying not to cry.

"We've got less than forty dollars."

"They'll never believe us."

"I know."

"What are we going to do?"

"Get the girls up. Get their shoes on," Randy said. "Don't make any noise. We might have to run out of here. God will help."

"Yes," I agreed. His confident words steadied me.

As I roused Courtney and her younger sister, Jessica, I heard Randy making his rounds once again, shouting out the windows from room to room.

Leaving baby Christopher to sleep in his crib, I told Courtney and Jessica to get dressed. Stifling any of their questions, I whispered what was happening. I hoped they didn't notice my warbling voice or shaking hands as I tried to help them dress.

The girls remained calm. They sat on the bed on either side of me, waiting for their father's next instructions. They trusted us. Now it was time for me to trust my heavenly Father.

Suddenly, I heard Randy at the bedroom door. I jumped up and pressed an ear to the door.

"We gotta get out of here," he said. "They just threw poison gas into one of the rooms, and I hear them on the roof, trying to get in."

"Okay. Tell me what to do." I swallowed and pushed back the tears. So far, God had protected us. The thieves had not been able to enter through any windows or the metal door, but I had never dreamed of them coming through the tin roof. My heart boomed with dread.

"I'll call for help one more time. But when I come back, be ready to run out the back door with me to the fence. The girls can climb over. After you get over, I'll hand Christopher to you. We have to run for it. The whole village is quiet. Seems like no one is here. I don't understand it."

"Okay, we're ready."

I turned around.

"When Daddy comes back," I whispered to the girls, "we'll run outside and climb over the fence."

"Okay, Mommy," they replied softly.

Climb over a fence? I asked myself. *With two little ones? How?*

Then I remembered the verse from the Psalms: "With my God I can scale any wall" (18:29).

Yes. God would help us.

"Girls, we gotta pray right now." We bowed our heads and prayed. Our help would come from the Lord and the

Lord alone. I remembered Psalm 44:6–7: "I do not trust in my bow; I do not count on my sword to save me. You are the one who gives us victory over our enemies."

After praying, we waited. The canine clamor became intermittent noises. Randy's voice trailed off into the night air. At any moment, Randy would come to the door, signaling for us to make a run for it. I felt ready for this adventure with a renewed surge of strength. God was our helper.

We continued to wait. At last there was a knock at the door. Our signal. I unlatched the lock and Randy pushed the door open. Pungent odors of the poison wafted into the chamber.

"We don't have to run. They're gone."

"What?"

"I've checked all around. There's not a sound anywhere. Afu and Igelina aren't barking anymore. No noise on the roof or at the window. They just left. Something scared them off. . . ."

Boom! Randy turned on his heels, waving his flashlight down the hallway toward the metal door.

"Don't worry." We heard a familiar voice through a front window. It was Steven, our neighbor. "I just saw some men running away from your house. Are you okay?"

The girls and I piled out of the room after Randy. When we entered the living room, I watched my husband unlock the big metal door and pull open its two wings.

"Whoa!" he cried out.

Our neighbor Steven entered.

"Look," my husband announced as he pointed at the base of the door. "I didn't lift up the bolt, but it didn't matter. The hole for the rod is so shallow that the door has never been secure. The thieves could have just pushed it open. We thought it was strong, but this door turned out to be our weakest link."

Randy and I laughed with relief. We had put our trust in a metal door that turned out to be useless. We had put our trust in our neighbors, but they had all gone to a burial that night, Steven explained.

My mind raced back to the moment the girls and I began praying. Our rescue did not come from our neighbors or a metal door. Our help came from the Lord. No bow, no sword, and no metal doors can save us from our enemies. Only God is able to rescue. It is a lesson I would remember many times during our missionary career.

A Voice From Heaven

MONICA CANE

It was morning and I was awake, but I was much too comfortable in my bed to get up. Instead, I stayed curled under my cozy covers with fluffy pillows all around me.

I kept my eyes closed and just listened to the sounds of the morning: the gurgling coffee percolating in the pot, birds chirping outside the window, and the *zip, zip* sound of my husband's duffel bag, letting me know he was getting ready to leave for work soon.

I felt a smidge guilty about being toasty warm under the covers, knowing he would have to fight cold weather and bumper-to-bumper traffic to get to work.

Apparently the guilt wasn't strong enough, however, because I pulled the covers over my head, wiggled my fingers and toes, and continued to lie there listening to the morning sounds.

I listened to the shuffling of my husband's bare feet in the kitchen and the swishing sound his pants made as he glided across the hall back into the bedroom to gather everything he would need for his day. I heard the click of the bathroom light and the squeak of the door as he opened and closed it. I recognized the gentle thud sound he makes when he plops into a chair to put on his socks and shoes while still trying his best to wake up and embrace the day.

With my eyes closed, I could not only hear the clear-cut sounds, but I could also visualize every detail of his morning routine. I found the image in my mind and all the sounds comforting.

A few minutes later, my husband's sounds died down. I assumed he was at the point of his morning routine where he sits in the living room drinking coffee and catching up on what important things happened on ESPN1 and ESPN2 during the night while he slept.

With my eyes still closed and the covers wrapped snuggly over my head, I began to hear another sound.

What was that?

It didn't sound like ESPN1 or 2 or any of the other countless sports channels that my husband might peruse before work. It was a different type of sound altogether, and it sounded close by.

It was a soft, muffled sound. I couldn't make out any of the words, but I could distinctly hear it. The more I listened, the more it sounded like praying was coming from the left side of the bed.

At that point I relaxed and assumed my husband had come back to our room and was kneeling by the bed, praying for the family, himself, and for the day before him. I waited silently for a few moments, wondering if I should open my eyes and let him know I was awake.

Not wanting to interrupt what seemed to be a very special prayer time, I decided I would just sneak a quick peek at him from beneath the covers. I quietly turned my head toward the left side of the bed where I heard the praying and carefully lifted a corner of the blanket. I cracked open my eyes, fully expecting to see my husband with his head bent, softly praying mighty prayers.

He wasn't there.

I popped open my eyes and snapped my head to the right to see if perhaps I'd just missed hearing him get up off his knees.

No one!

I snatched my glasses from the bed stand and put them on. Perhaps my husband was walking out of the room and I could catch a glimpse of him. But he wasn't there, either. Where did he go? Was he already on his way to work? Why didn't I hear the door shut? When did he stop praying? He was the one praying, right?

I figured there had to be a reasonable explanation for the fact that I didn't hear my husband leave and also for the muffled praying sound I had heard.

Still a little stunned by it all, I decided to reach out to the only reliable resource I knew of that could possibly have the answer to this unexpected early morning occurrence. I began to call on God in prayer, but before I could even fully pose the question, a clear, solid answer overwhelmed me: *The Spirit intercedes for the saints.*

A chill washed over me as I considered the possibility that it might not have been my husband praying beside our bed, but the Spirit of the living God interceding on our behalf just as His Word says.

When my husband returned from work that evening, he confirmed that he had not been praying by the bed in the morning. I couldn't believe it. I was still trying to justify somehow that I had heard praying by the bed. It is one thing to read God's Word and choose to believe it, and it's another thing entirely to experience it firsthand in a supernatural way.

As I mulled these thoughts, I once again was overwhelmed with the revelation of Romans 8:27: "The Spirit intercedes for the saints" (ESV).

As a believer in Christ, I suppose I shouldn't have been so surprised. But I was surprised. I still am surprised.

That morning, not ready to get out of bed, I was listening to the sounds around me—the sounds of my husband preparing for work and the many other sounds of my household.

In the midst of it all, God revealed a truth that I may have taken for granted prior to that morning: There is a great yet unheard sound going on around believers every day at all times. It's the sound of the Spirit interceding for your needs and for mine.

Holy Electricity

DELORES E. TOPLIFF

When my son Andrew was three years old, we learned through a routine medical checkup that he had a heart murmur. Our doctor said not to be alarmed because many children have this condition, but it needed to be watched. Andrew was our adorable, chunky firstborn with dark ringlets. How could anything be wrong with his wonderfully strong body?

This report added a black cloud to our horizon. Relatives on my side of the family had experienced serious heart problems. Mother's baby brother had died at six months from a heart defect. I had a congenital cardiac block and eventually a series of pacemakers.

I drove home that day with my world in slow motion. Andrew played with our neighbor's cute puppy in our living room while I attacked some ironing. I turned our radio to a classic music station. As I listened, I cried out to God. "Please don't let this be true. But if it is, please help us walk through it."

Suddenly I became aware of what was playing on the radio. I'd previously had little appreciation for Bach. But as I ironed sweeping arcs across my husband's shirt, Bach's Fourth Brandenburg Concerto became God's promise to me. The recurring, majestic theme reminded me of the steadfast beating heart of God. Its music flowed into me. I sensed the assurance that God's own heart would keep my son's heart beating, too.

I had other concerns besides Andrew's health. Because of stress, my husband resigned his teaching job. He asked me to take our two young sons back to my hometown while he figured things out.

After suggesting many alternative plans that did not interest him, I finally packed the car. Within a month I found good work and a reliable baby-sitter.

Soon it was time again for Andrew's yearly checkup. The first doctor checked our son while nurses prepped him for an electrocardiogram.

"You can feel the murmur externally," I heard one nurse say.

After the EKG, the doctors told me we had a serious problem: patent ductus arteriosus, or PDA. This is an opening between the aorta and pulmonary artery that normally closes at birth. They said this condition is sometimes undetected until a seemingly healthy child drops dead during normal activity.

If it wasn't surgically repaired, Andrew could die before he was twelve.

They scheduled an appointment at a children's hospital for additional tests, but there was a three-month waiting list.

From the doctor's appointment, we headed straight to church. Two weeks earlier God had impressed me to join a Wednesday night Bible study at a friend's church. They were studying healing and the Holy Spirit. I was thankful the Bible study was that night. I needed God's help.

When I dropped the boys off at the nursery and walked into the meeting room, my friend wasn't there yet and I didn't know anyone else. I sank into a pew. Trauma must have shown on my face as a woman approached and said, "Is everything all right? You're white as a sheet. How can we help?"

I explained our medical report. She said several of the people had just attended a retreat on healing prayer—would I let them pray for Andrew?

"Of course," I replied.

I believed that God *could* heal, but thought we must be good enough to deserve it. How could anyone be good enough for that?

Nonetheless, not wanting to offend these new friends, I agreed. I got Andrew from the nursery and put him on my lap so he wouldn't be alarmed. And then they prayed for both of us.

I didn't sense immediate results, but I did appreciate everyone's obvious care. They let me borrow a grocery bag full of books on healing and the Holy Spirit.

I settled into a pattern for the next three months with my little family. Work. Take care of the kids. Pray lots, and look forward to Wednesday night Bible studies. I began daring to hope God might do something, though I still felt undeserving. During these months, every night after my boys were asleep, I laid loving hands on Andrew's chest and prayed. Each time I did, I felt his lurching heart. And each time I cried.

One day I read one of the books I had borrowed, Agnes Sanford's *Healing Light*. She said God's answers do not depend on our deserving them, but upon God's power and unchanging principles. He answers prayers because *He* is good, not because we are. She compared divine power to electricity, pointing out that our homes are wired for electricity, but if we insist on understanding all the workings of circuitry, amperage, wattage, and voltage before we turn on the light switch, we might stay in the dark.

She added that we should envision God's love coming to the person who needs healing to correct everything broken and incomplete. As much as I loved my son, I began to understand that God loved him even more than I did. And I relinquished my fears and doubts.

That night I laid hands on Andrew's chest, praying the new kind of prayer. I thanked God for His perfect love that lets nothing imperfect stand in its way.

Then I experienced something no one had mentioned. Strong waves of pulsating energy, like warm currents of electricity, flowed from the room, through my hands, and into my son. This lasted for five minutes before Andrew sighed and turned over into deeper sleep.

The night before my son's 8 a.m. hospital appointment, I had to work until 2 a.m., so I was exhausted when Andrew and I arrived at the medical center to undergo tests and meet a panel of nine doctors.

Besides testing times and a thirty-minute lunch break, we spent all day in a waiting room filled with sadness and parents with children in all stages of heart disease. Some children had blue skin tones, others gray, but all were there for testing. Around five o'clock, I was one of the first parents called in.

Nine doctors sat around the long conference table with Andrew's medical records spread out before them.

"Mrs. Topliff, we cannot account for this," a doctor said. "Your internists and the June electrocardiogram indicated clinical patent ductus arteriosus. We might conclude the testing equipment was faulty that day, except the nurses' notes confirm the condition by external examination. They could feel the lurching. Today, however, your son is in the normal zone. We see minor valve stricture, but he'll out-grow that."

Exhausted and steeled to face hardship, I could not comprehend these words.

"How do I need to limit Andrew physically? What other restrictions are necessary?" I asked.

"None," they chorused.

"When should he be re-examined?"

"Just normal yearly checkups."

Since I clearly wasn't getting it, another doctor leaned forward and smiled. "Mrs. Topliff, though Andrew had the condition, he doesn't have it now. No surgery is needed. Your son is in the normal zone."

Still not fully comprehending, I thanked the doctors and left as the next frightened parent walked in. Drained by the prolonged tension, I held my four-year-old's hand while we walked to our car.

Andrew was a very ordinary four-year-old who loved sticks and frogs and rocks and mud puddles. Besides often loudly singing "Jesus loves me, this I know," he didn't normally do anything spiritual. But now he tugged at my hand and pointed at the top of the twelve-story parking garage. "Mommy, why is an angel on top of that building?"

"What? Where?" I asked, head swiveling as cold chills gripped my spine.

"There, Mommy. On top of that building. And it's smiling at us."

Like any overwhelmed mother, I burst into tears.

"I don't know why an angel is up there smiling at us," I said. "But I do know God helped us today."

That miracle changed our lives.

Andrew remembers the angel, and that experience helped him know God personally cares for him.

The miracle showed me that God loves helping everyone, maybe especially moms raising kids. But it also made me keep looking for the God who is "more." If He saves us, forgives us without our deserving it, and heals us, what other things does He have for us to discover?

As we walk with Him, He continues encouraging us. He's eager to show us more parts of himself through answered prayer and other adventures He has waiting right around the corner.

About the Contributors

Marlene Anderson is a licensed mental health counselor and the author of *A Love So Great, A Grief So Deep*. She is a speaker who has worked in clinical and educational settings and is a member of the Northwest Christian Writers Association and Speakers Bureau.

James Stuart Bell owns Whitestone Communications, a literary development agency, and is the compiler of this volume and over thirty others of its kind.

Timothy J. Burt is a practicing therapist in the area of Christian counseling and hails from Easton, Pennsylvania. He greatly enjoys his three grown children and four grandchildren.

Monica Cane is a freelance writer and founder of A Breath of Inspiration Ministry. Her books include *A Journey to*

Healing: Life After SIDS; *A Breath of Inspiration*; *CJ's Peace: The Prodigal's Progress*; and *The Lost Coin*. She resides in Northern California.

Betty Johnson Dalrymple, writer of devotions and personal experience stories, is a contributor to numerous inspirational books. She participates in Bible studies, plays golf, and spends fun time with her husband, Bob, and their large blended family.

Sally Edwards Danley lives in Kansas City, where she helps writers and works with prayer and recovery ministries. She enjoys writing devotionals and personal experiences for anthologies.

Scoti Springfield Domeij, a Gold Star mother, loves her sons, Kristoffer and Kyle. Sergeant First Class Kristoffer Domeij, elite Army Ranger, was killed in action in Afghanistan on his fourteenth special operations deployment. Scoti helps single parents process grief to embrace new life. She blogs at www.scotidomeij.wordpress.com.

Dale L. Dragomir has been a pastor for more than thirty years. He is a graduate of Asbury Theological Seminary and currently serves the congregation of Wilmore Christian Church in Kentucky.

Annette M. Eckart, founder of Bridge for Peace, www.bridgeforpeace.org, leads mission teams worldwide and preaches at international conferences. She teaches people to apply God's Word and get results that glorify Jesus Christ.

Loretta Eidson completed four years of study with the Christian Writers Guild and has stories published in an anthology and several other books, including two of James Bell's previous compilations.

George Ferrer is a manager for Catholic Cemeteries and lives on Long Island in New York. He has taught adult Sunday school for thirty years and is an active volunteer in many aspects of Christian education in the area.

G. L. Francis is a Midwestern writer, artist, and Jane-of-many-trades.

Joyce Gatton received the coveted Best Actress of Washington High School, 1969 award. She loves her grandchildren, working with her husband, Stan, and leading the Soul Sisters' Ministry at her church in Kansas City, Kansas.

Judy Hampton is a popular conference speaker and author. Her testimony has aired several times on the *Focus on the Family* radio broadcast. She has written three full-length books and hundreds of articles.

Bob Haslam has been a pastor, missionary, and editor. Currently he ministers in many ways, including teaching people how to write for publication.

Christine Henderson is a realtor by day and a writer by night. Her life-inspired stories about family issues have been published in several anthologies. You can also find her writings in *Ruminate Magazine, The Secret Place,* and *Berry Blue Haiku.*

Linda Howton attended first grade in a two-room schoolhouse in Table Rock, Oregon. Now retired in Kansas, she still enjoys the country life with her husband, David, and three cats.

Walter B. Huckaby has served in the U.S. Navy in aviation electronics and in local churches as pastor and educational director. He has also taught in private schools for eighteen years.

Jeanie Jacobson has enjoyed various careers, from programming computers to working with special-needs children. Her motto remains "God is faithful." She and her husband, Jake, live in Bellevue, Nebraska.

P. R. Jaramillo has a master's degree in counseling. She's written self-help books and conducts healing from personal loss workshops. Her latest book is a historical overview of the American Southwest.

Cheryl Christensen Johnston is an inspirational real-life storywriter and serves her central Florida community as president of Brandon Christian Writers and as Christian education director at Plant City Church of God.

Sheryl K. Jones served as a missionary with her husband in Cameroon, Africa. Currently she serves as a pastor's wife, is a mother of five children, and works as a speech therapist.

Delores Christian Liesner is a writer and speaker and serves as God's delivery girl. Delores lives life passionately as a twenty-first-century grandma. Check out her blog "Be The Miracle!" at Deloresliesner.com or contact her by email: delores7faith@yahoo.com.

Susan A. J. Lyttek, author of the cozy mystery *Homeschooling Can Be Murder* and the upcoming *Killer Field Trip,* writes early mornings before homeschooling, and she enjoys coaching young writers. She and Gary, married since 1983, live near our nation's capital.

John C. Mannone was nominated three times for the Pushcart Prize and has been published in *The Baltimore Review, Tipton Poetry Journal,* and *The Pedestal.* He teaches college physics in Tennessee. Visit The Art of Poetry at http://jcmannone .wordpress.com.

Alice M. McGhee lives in Colorado with her husband, Ken, and dog, Precious. She has published a book titled *Peace in the Midst of Pain* and has contributed to several devotional books.

Martha Nelson is a published poet, songwriter, drummer, wife of sixty-four years, mother, and grandmother. She has seen God do many wonderful things in her life.

Judy Parrott writes inspirational nonfiction. She is widowed with three sons, eight grandchildren, and five great-grandchildren. She has a nursing background and two years of seminary training.

Carolyn D. Poindexter enjoys freelance writing and amateur photography. A church administrator by day, her nighttime passion is working on her first manuscript, *When It's Time to Say Good-Bye,* a story of emotional healing after losing her only son to cancer.

Trish Propson owns Cornerstone Communications Company (www.cornerstonecomm.org) and directs Rekenekt, offering restoration to families. She has authored a mother/daughter discipleship program, *Raising Little Women of God.*

Marty Prudhomme is a freelance writer who has written and taught Bible studies for twenty years. She serves as the Louisiana vice president of leaders' training for Aglow International.

Janice Rice pastors with her husband and four children in Oregon. She is passionate about leading worship and missions. Her hobbies include long-distance running and writing.

M. Jeanette Sharp is a multi-published writer. Her latest is a biography, *The Paint Man: My Life in Living Color.* She lives in Edmond, Oklahoma, with her husband, Jim, and their fur-person, Maggie Sue.

Ingrid Shelton is a retired teacher and librarian. She is a freelance writer and loves to grow organic vegetables and fruit. Walking, volunteering at care homes, and reading are her other hobbies.

Kelly J. Stigliano has been a writer and speaker for over twenty-five years. She and her husband, Jerry, enjoy life in Orange Park, Florida. To learn more, visit www.kellystigliano .com.

Margaret Ann Stimatz works as a mental health therapist in Helena, Montana.

Jan Dixon Sykes has an opinion column in her county newspaper outside Kansas City, where she lives with her husband. Jan manages their rental properties and the Dixon Ranch.

Delores E. Topliff lives near Minneapolis. She loves Jesus, family, grandchildren, writing, college teaching, mission trips, travel, and her new farm with apple trees and cows.

Deb Wuethrich is a staff writer for *The Tecumseh Herald* in Tecumseh, Michigan. She is a 2003 recipient of an Amy Award of Outstanding Merit and has contributed to several anthologies.

Martin Ziegner has been a general dentist for over forty years in the western suburbs of Chicago, Illinois. He has two adult children, three dachshunds, and a parrot.

James Stuart Bell is a Christian publishing veteran and the owner of Whitestone Communications, a literary development agency. He is the editor of many story collections, including the CUP OF COMFORT, LIFE SAVORS, and the GOD ENCOUNTERS series, as well as the coauthor of numerous books in the COMPLETE IDIOT'S GUIDE series. He and his family live in West Chicago, Illinois.

Read More About the Supernatural

This fascinating look at the supernatural world offers a compilation of more than forty true stories of miraculous provision, encounters with angels and demons, near-death experiences, and incredible rescues. You'll marvel at how God and His angels are working behind the scenes to protect and guide us.

Angels, Miracles, and Heavenly Encounters compiled by James Stuart Bell

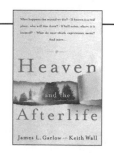

In a candid, biblical examination of the world beyond this life, bestselling author and pastor Jim Garlow helps you sort out fact from fiction when it comes to what's "on the other side." The afterlife is very real, but not everything you hear about it is. Get the answers you need to decide for yourself.

Heaven and the Afterlife by James L. Garlow with Keith Wall

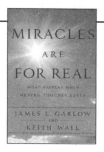

Jim Garlow and Keith Wall share amazing stories of God at work in our world, examine biblical teaching about miracles, and provide trustworthy information that will boost your faith. Whether you need a miracle today or you want to understand how to recognize the supernatural when you see it, this is your inspiring guide.

Miracles Are for Real by James L. Garlow and Keith Wall

BETHANYHOUSE